EXCHANGING MY DISABILITY FOR GOD'S ABILITY

I Am Free to Be Me

Joy Ani

Sunesis Ministries Ltd

Exchanging My Disability for God's Ability: I Am Free to Be Me

Copyright © 2013 Joy Ani.

The right of Joy Ani to be identified as author of this work has been asserted by her in accordance with the Copyright, Designs, and Patents Act 1988.

The author guarantees all contents are original and do not infringe upon the legal rights of any other person or work. All rights reserved. No part of this publication may be reproduced or transmitted in any form or by any means, electronic or mechanical, including photocopy, recording, or any information storage and retrieval system, without permission in writing from the author.

ISBN: 978-0-9566864-8-0

Scripture quotations marked NKJV are taken from the Holy Bible, New King James Version, copyright © 1982 by Thomas Nelson, Inc. Used by permission. All rights reserved.

Scripture quotations marked KJV are from the Holy Bible, King James Version.

Scripture quotations marked NLT are taken from the Holy Bible, New Living Translation, copyright © 1996, 2004, 2007 by Tyndale House Foundation. Used by permission of Tyndale House Publishers, Inc., Carol Stream, Illinois 60188. All rights reserved.

Scripture quotations marked NIV are taken from The Holy Bible, New International Version®, NIV® Copyright © 1973, 1978, 1984, 2011 by Biblica, Inc.™ Used by permission. All rights reserved worldwide.
Scripture quotations marked AMP are taken from the Amplified® Bible, Copyright © 1954, 1958, 1962, 1964, 1965, 1987 by The Lockman Foundation. Used by permission. www.Lockman.org

Published by Sunesis Ministries Ltd
Email: info@stuartpattico.com
Website: www.stuartpattico.com

The views expressed in this book are solely those of the author and do not necessarily reflect the views of the publisher, and the publisher hereby disclaims any responsibility for them. The author accepts sole legal responsibility for the contents of this book.

Disclaimer

The information in this book represents the views and opinions of the author as at the date of publication. This book is not intended to be a source or resource for advice on health or human rights, but it is part of the author's story of her journey of transition from negative and limiting thinking to a radical understanding of her situation through the eyes of God and not man. Therefore, the information in this book is a source of general information to promote an awareness of deafness and disabilities.

Clarification of Terms Used

For the purpose of this book, reference to:

EXCHANGING MY DISABILITY FOR GOD'S ABILITY

i. A 'disabled person' – refers to a person with one or more illness, disease, emotional or mobility issue that affects them by limiting their ability to think, communicate, use their senses, their limbs, and/or co-ordinate their body movements or perform one or more activity unassisted and with ease.

ii. A 'deaf person' – refers to a person who falls within the spectrum of deafness, from mild to being profoundly deaf. It includes pre-lingual, post-lingual, deaf-blind and acquired whether British Sign Language (BSL) is their first or preferred language or not.

Dedication

This book is dedicated to God my Father, my creator who knew me before I was formed in my mother's womb. You are indeed a loving Father. God, I can't do without You.

To my Lord Jesus, the lover of my soul – I know this very well because without Your love for me I would have drowned in hopelessness – You are always there to give me hope. I will forever love You and tell others about Your faithfulness.

To the Holy Spirit, what can I say? You are my helper, my comforter, my counsellor and friend; when I feel like giving up I can hear You whispering in my ears that the Father has not finished with me yet. You are indeed a friend! I will forever honour You.

To all the deaf and disabled people in the world, I say 'Arise and Shine' and let your dreams also 'Arise and Shine'.

This book is also dedicated to all those who took part in the London Paralympics. Those men, women and young adults of courage showed the world their determination, tenacity and passion. For many, the realisation of their dream was not easy task but an uphill endeavour. In the end, in the midst of the overwhelming euphoria, many were able to achieve their dreams.

Finally, I wish to dedicate this book to all the parents, siblings and other carers, guardians and support service providers to deaf and disabled children, young adults and adults. Many give selflessly and are able to separate their own desires and dreams from those of the person they are caring for. These are people who have made it their goal to at least empower the person they are caring for with life skills and, where possible, recognise their potential. They encourage, motivate and provide or utilise services that will help the person in their care to realise and release their potential, and in doing so achieve their dreams.

Thank you.

Foreword

The subject of this book, 'Exchanging My Disability for God's Ability', is very dear to me.

I have had the opportunity to work with and support many deaf and disabled children and adults over the past few years. I respect, admire, applaud, empathise and sympathise with many. Many others I have applauded as they have challenged my initial mind-set; now they have inspired me and I have learned to appreciate and love them.

For most deaf and disabled people, one of the things they have in common is the struggle with their identity – knowing and appreciating who they are and what they are capable of. Others who have accepted their deafness or disability have embarked on a journey to find out who they really are. Each person has the right to take advantage of opportunities available to them, including knowing what they are entitled to under the Equality Act 2010 and Human Rights legislations.

As you read this book, if you are deaf or disabled, be ready to have your perception of yourself and your situation challenged. You will need to reflect on and review your past, present and future dreams. If you have been made weak by your deafness or disability up to now, you have picked a book that will pick you up. It will give you hope and inspire you to move on with your life, confident that you can make a difference in your community or society.

Don't give up. I think this book can revive your desires, give you hope, and encourage and inspire you to improve your life.

If you do not consider yourself to be deaf or disabled, what thoughts do you have about deaf and disabled people? This book will give you an insight into their world and how you can enable them to realise their dreams of being viable citizens with economic worth.

Deborah Essien

Coordinator of Talking Hands Fellowship

Acknowledgements

I would like to thank my family for their unending support and encouragement:

To Ufeli, my beloved daughter, I will never forget the night you cried and prayed with me and said, "Mummy, if 'ears' as a spare part were within my reach, I would have given everything to get them for you." My dear, be assured God is doing a new thing.

To my dear daughter Natasha, I am immensely grateful for your words of encouragement: "Mum, God will do it in His own time." Those words were highly appreciated; they made a difference. Thanks for your frankness.

To my son, like your namesake who was a man after God's heart, King David, you are indeed a son after my heart; your support, caring nature and words of encouragement have been a tower of strength to me. Those words of encouragement urged me to write this book.

To my honourable husband, thanks for your constant prayers and your prayer requests on my behalf. Thank you for not getting fed up of having to repeat yourself several times until I have heard and understood what you've said. I also thank you for loving me just the way I am. I am forever grateful.

To Pastor Raphael Olurotimi, you are indeed an intercessor. Not only do you pray for me when we meet, but on occasions I have seen you in my dreams praying for me. Please be confident that your prayers have been answered.

To all the Pastors, Ministers and friends who pray fervently for God to heal me, be assured that God has answered your prayers.

To all my brothers and sisters in Christ and friends who are still finding it hard to understand the loss of my hearing: I identify with your shock and I do understand that it is hard on you as well, because you constantly have to repeat yourselves until I can make sense of what you say. The Lord is our strength.

My appreciation also goes to Marie-Pearl Addo-Afful who did the initial proofreading of the manuscript. You have been a blessing and an encourager. May your dreams come to pass speedily, in Jesus' name.

To my able and talented wise editor, Tola Awe. Your patience and understanding are inspiring. I appreciate your contribution. You are a great blessing to this project. I am holding onto the prophecy you gave me, "A ministry is born." Together we shall celebrate the goodness of God in the ministry.

Lastly, but not the least, my able Team Leader Mr Thomas Okech, you are one in a million. Your support and encouragement are highly appreciated (I regularly hear your voice saying, "Joy, you can do it!"). Your understanding of my hearing loss was amazing; you never treated me differently, instead you gave me attention and time to come to terms with my loss and you made my job easier for me. May the good Lord support you and be there for you in your times of need.

Contents

DISCLAIMER & CLARIFICATION OF TERMS   3

DEDICATION   5

FOREWORD   7

ACKNOWLEDGEMENTS   9

INTRODUCTION   15

CHAPTER 1 - This is my story   21

CHAPTER 2 - The diagnosis   25

CHAPTER 3 - The disability and me   29

CHAPTER 4 - Be calm   35

CHAPTER 5 - What is the way forward?   45

CHAPTER 6 - What do you have?   53

CHAPTER 7 - Change the way you think   61

CHAPTER 8 - Forgiveness is the way to wholeness   69

CHAPTER 9 - Confessing your way out of disabling and limiting thoughts with God's enabling and empowering promises   75

CHAPTER 10 - Use what you have   83

CHAPTER 11 - Developing strategies for coping with your deafness or disability 87

CHAPTER 12 - Who are you? 91

CHAPTER 13 - Believe and develop a winning attitude 101

CHAPTER 14 - Hope against hope 105

CHAPTER 15 - Move on – let go and let God 113

CHAPTER 16 - What's next? 117

CHAPTER 17 - Deaf awareness 121

CHAPTER 18 - Church attitudes towards deafness and disability 127

CHAPTER 19 - Some of the world's famous people who are deaf or disabled 135

Further Information 151

Some names and email addresses of organisations providing training and information for the deaf and disabled communities

ABOUT THE AUTHOR 153

Introduction

The initial purpose of writing this book was to encourage others who have been on a journey of transition from being 'hearing' to being 'deaf'. Then I realised that what I was writing would also be helpful to people who are 'disabled'. The commonality of deafness with some disabilities is that both are hidden. If a deaf person doesn't wear their hearing aid no one, at a glance, will realise that the person is disabled. Other hidden disabilities include: asthma, Crohn's disease, colitis, sickle cell anaemia, diabetes, cancer, and there are so many others. Therefore, most of those who are deaf or have a hidden disability are viewed with suspicion. Many experience rejection and discrimination in the wider community and society as a consequence of their disability. Some deaf and disabled people who have a hidden disability choose to carry a badge or card that states the name of the disability, and in some cases who to contact in an emergency. This book will touch on how deafness and disabilities can affect people's lives.

Manufacturers, public and private sector service providers, including local and central government, educational institutions, financial institutions, retailers and churches, will also benefit from this book.

This book is for you if you are deaf or if you have any type of disability, visible or hidden. Is your disability stopping you from being who you are meant to be? This book will hopefully encourage you to realise that you can be who you are meant to be, and reassure you of the unfailing love and promises of God.

We are the human race, one race, with the ability to communicate and relate to each other, but instead sometimes we avoid people who are different to us when we should embrace and celebrate the differences of others, especially when it pertains to 'disabilities'.

This book is also for church leaders. In my opinion, though more churches are opening their doors, few are opening their arms to provide support for deaf and disabled people. Therefore this book serves as a wake-up call to church leaders, in general. They need to do more to include and integrate people with deafness and disabilities into their programmes, and thereby enable them to find the love and acceptance they need to fulfil the purpose of God for their lives. The body of Christ in general needs to demonstrate the nature of the God who loves and cares for all people, including the deaf and disabled (John 3:16). This group are part of the 'flock' of the church and should be appreciated, supported and encouraged to realise their potential in Him (see Philippians 4:13), utilise their gifts and to become Christ's disciples and disciplers (Matthew 28:18-20).

The culture and attitudes encountered in some churches has had a negative impact on deaf and disabled people, to the point that their experience has made them reluctant to go to church. Others feel that many of the leaders and members will not welcome them or appreciate their presence or difference, or make the necessary specific adjustments required. This results in many deaf and disabled people missing out on intimacy with God, though He wants them to know and relate to Him. Some, unfortunately, develop negative attitudes and mind-sets about God, the Church and the Word of God, and ultimately look elsewhere for acceptance, identity, belonging and satisfaction.

Retailers and other service providers will also benefit from serving deaf and disabled customers better. They may already provide written information in Braille or large-print, but with the current advancements in technology further adaptations are available, such as 'text to speech' technology. Many computers have inbuilt software which reads texts including emails and documents, describes products, venues and events, and now mobile phones have the technology to read text messages aloud. The retailer may need to provide their information on the specific format that complies with the available software.

Serving the deaf and disabled communities is not just about providing a ramp for wheelchair users or providing large print text for the visually challenged. Deaf and disabled people may require specific adaptations to be made, which should be reflected in the method by which the service is promoted and supplied. An awareness of the specific group of people, their culture and needs is essential.

It would be wrong to group all deaf people in the same category, because some deaf people would not consider themselves disabled but as a linguistic/language minority person. The people in this group are able to: lip-read, read English text, write, and comprehend better than other people.

For example, some deaf people cannot read, speak or write legibly or grammatically, and will need the service of a British Sign Language communicator. This service needs to be at an appropriate level of proficiency, capable of facilitating communication between the respective parties, usually at NVQ Level 3 and above, to Interpreter level.

Another example: A blind person has a stick which may be white or white with another colour, denoting that the individual has additional disability. The person may need a guide dog or a guide (person) to assist on a daily basis. They may require written information in Braille or large-print, but further adaptations are now available, such as the 'text to speech' technology I've referred to. Many computers have inbuilt software which reads text and mobile phones have the technology to read messages aloud. Manufacturers, public and private sector service providers should provide information concerning their products and services in formats that suit deaf and disabled customers, and utilise technological aids to communication.

Although the marginalisation of deaf and disabled people from society or the community where they live or work may not be intentional, there is no acceptable or justifiable reason for this situation to continue in these days of technological advancements, and of awareness and celebration of diversity. Costs should be factored in at the planning stages of any programme or project to comply with the necessary adaptations recommended in the Equality Act 2010 and Human Rights legislations. This book aims, through the insight I've gained on my journey, to offer a way of bridging the gap and encouraging those who have experienced discrimination to have hope.

I was born hearing and now I know what it is to be deaf. I am learning to lip-read while using the residual hearing that I have. It's not easy, but one thing I am sure of is this: I have a hope, I am a child of God and I know that God loves me and that He has a plan for me. I am sure of this!

CHAPTER 1

This is My Story

I am a child of God, He loves me, He has a plan and a future for me (see Jeremiah 29:11).

I am a wife, mother, Senior Benefits Officer and a Sunday School teacher. I am a busy person. Meeting people, attending meetings and using the telephone are all important aspects of my work.

Imagine picking up a phone and not hearing the dialling tone, or you dial a number and then think that you do not have a connection because you can't hear anything.

Imagine the light indicator on your phone is 'flashing' to inform you that you have a call, but when you pick up the phone you think no one is there.

I have tried to remember when the sound of traffic became quiet. Sounds in general became less intrusive. Though the pace of life is fast, busy and hectic at times, the sounds I heard did not reflect all the hustle and bustle of such times. It seemed like people were suddenly talking softly or mumbling. What a conundrum!

"Sorry, can you repeat that again, please?"

"Pardon, I am sorry, I didn't catch what you said."

"Sorry, I missed what you said."

"Sorry, I don't understand what you are saying."

"Can you speak louder, please?"

"Can you speak a little slower, please?"

Then the puzzled looks and glances that seem to say:

"Is she alright?" or "What's her problem?"

"Poor thing!" or whatever...

Have you been there? So have I.

What about the times you misheard and mistook a word like "fish" for "finish".

Or have you tried to lip-read and thought:

"Did she say try or dry?"

"Did my baby mean 'ate' or 'eight'?"

"Did he mean 'alter' – change – or 'altar' – in church?"

Dear Lord, context, context, context!

Then I would be exasperated: "Not again!... What an embarrassment!... This is embarrassing!"

I became aware that something was wrong; but what?

"Why am I not interacting with people like I used to? Something is different; is it me or them?"

I decided to go to the GP for a hearing test, but my GP referred me to the audiology department in an Ears, Eyes, Nose and Throat hospital.

While waiting for the appointment I became anxious and confused, depressed and sometimes distraught too. I didn't want to think that I may be deaf, but I was also acknowledging that it was a possibility.

I got the appointment, at last. I went to the hospital and the hearing test was conducted. It revealed that I was indeed losing my hearing.

As you read my story I will make reference to God's Word and how it has helped me and continues to help and lead me throughout this journey.

"The Lord is my shepherd; I shall not want" (Psalm 23:1, NKJV) has become a very profound Bible verse for me.

I pray that as you start to turn over your disability to God, you will begin to receive His ability because He promises that "I can do all things through Christ who strengthens me" (Philippians 4:13, NKJV.

For all of you who are either deaf or disabled, or deaf and disabled, I hope and pray that you will find comfort, inspiration and encouragement reading this book.

Even with your deafness/disability YOU CAN aspire to greatness!

CHAPTER 2

The Diagnosis

The test revealed that I was losing my hearing, enough to be considered 'deafened' or some would say 'hearing impaired' or 'deaf'.

"What?! Deaf?! ME?!"

Then a part of me thought that I had definitely misheard. My shock was too much to comprehend the diagnosis.

"What?! No! Not me. When? How did it happen? Why me?"

Maybe you thought this or you may have exclaimed it.

"I am disabled? No! I will not accept that. I am not disabled. I AM NOT… am I?"

Have you been there? I have.

I wonder if you have breathed a sigh of relief at the realisation that you were not and are not crazy, not losing your mind, only losing your hearing. It is all a mixed blessing, isn't it?

If you haven't taken that sigh of relief yet, why not do so now.

Maybe like me you asked yourself questions:

"Disabled!? What does it mean to be disabled?"

"How will it affect me?"

"Can I work or not?"

"How do I explain this to my family?"

"How do I explain this to my manager and colleagues?"

"What will they think or say?"

"Will they say or think it's my fault?"

"Will I lose my job?"

"Where can I go for help?"

"Do I have any rights?"

"What's next?"

"What can I do?"

Questions, questions, questions… Have you been there? I have.

STOP! Slow down and calm down.

The words that confirmed my fears were the most devastating words I had ever heard. Initially, I refused to accept them and continued to live in denial, struggling to cope with everyday conversations and praying secretly for God to heal me. In return for my healing, I promised God that I would give testimonies of His goodness and faithfulness. I went further, I actually promised Him that if He would heal me of my hearing loss I would write a book in honour of His name. I am still praying and expecting God to heal me.

"He comforts us in all our troubles so that we can comfort others. When they are troubled, we will be able to give them the same comfort God has given us."
2 Corinthians 1:4 (NLT)

The comfort and reassurance I have received from God and some friends and relations enables me to extend a hand of love, comfort and reassurance to you.

CHAPTER 3

The Disability and Me

What does it mean to be disabled? I was not sure, I was confused. I felt angry and guilty, and I couldn't think clearly, but in the middle of my confused state a Bible verse came to mind.

"See, I lay a stone in Zion, a chosen and precious cornerstone, and the one who trusts in him will never be put to shame." 1 Peter 2:6 (NIV)

God says that His children will not be put to shame. Well, at the time I wasn't sure about that! If God says that I won't be shamed what does He mean? He means what He says!

So I decided to research the meaning of the word 'shame'. I found out that amongst other things 'shame' means: disgrace, embarrassment, dishonour and humiliation.

I was born hearing and now I have become deaf, yet God says that I will not be ashamed!

But the most important words are "THE ONE WHO TRUSTS IN HIM will never be put to shame."

I wonder if you made the same mistake I did earlier? I misquoted the Bible verse. Did you notice that I omitted those all-important words, 'the one who trusts in him'? It is not those who trust in themselves or others, but ONLY those who trust in 'him'. Who is 'him' – this "stone in Zion", this "chosen and precious cornerstone"? Jesus.

When I compared myself with others I experienced shame. However, I have come to the understanding that whatever God allows is for a reason, a purpose and a season (however short or long), and He will give me the strength, conviction, ability and wisdom to depend on Him to overcome this difficulty.

To receive the promised covering from God I have to trust and believe His Word. The Bible says that without faith it is impossible to please God (Hebrews 11:6). Therefore, knowing the Word of God, believing that His promises are true and drawing close to Him are important attributes to develop.

This part of my journey has made me realise that whether we admit it or not, we have our own appreciation or understanding of what is right and wrong, acceptable and unacceptable, because our value judgments are the basis of the shame we experience and the degree of influence this emotion has on us.

Where does shame come from?

Shame is the consequence of sin and errors we make – it is an act (e.g. John 8:1-11).

Shame may occur as a consequence of an abusive and/or painful incident (e.g. 2 Samuel 13:1-20).

Shame may occur as a reaction to an uncomfortable or awkward feeling (e.g. Acts 3:1-8).

Shame is an emotion which if not controlled and dealt with can overtake us and cause us to behave in a manner that can be destructive and inhibiting.

Let's look at other Bible verses...

To receive the promised covering and protection from God I have to trust Him and believe His Word.

"Because the Sovereign Lord helps me, I will not be disgraced. Therefore have I set my face like flint, and I know I will not be put to shame." Isaiah 50:7 (NIV)

"The Lord knows the days of the upright, and their inheritance shall be forever. They shall not be ashamed in the evil time, and in the days of famine they shall be satisfied." Psalm 37:18-19 (NKJV)

"Do not be afraid; you will not be put to shame. Do not fear disgrace; you will not be humiliated. You will forget the shame of your youth and remember no more the reproach of your widowhood." Isaiah 54:4 (NIV)

"Anyone who trusts in him will never be disgraced." Romans 10:11 (NLT)

"Instead of your shame you will receive a double portion, and instead of disgrace you will rejoice in your inheritance. And so you will inherit a double portion in your land, and everlasting joy will be yours." Isaiah 61:7 (NIV)

"Whoever dwells in the shelter of the Most High will rest in the shadow of the Almighty. I will say of the Lord, 'He is my refuge and my fortress, my God, in whom I trust." Psalm 91:1-2 (NIV)

Once again, remember that shame is an emotion; it affects different people differently. The antidote for shame is love and acceptance. The greatest antidote is God: He is love. See Him at work in and through your situation. He knows the plans He has for you, and He may want to use you to be the catalyst or springboard for change and innovation.

Therefore, knowing the Word of God, believe that His promises are true, and by drawing close to Him realise that there are important attributes to develop.

For example:

- Braille was invented by Louise Braille in 1924 for blind people and recently text to speech software has been invented for visually challenged people to use.

- Hearing aids were invented for and used by people who are deaf.

- After much debate, sign language is used to facilitate communication between deaf and hearing people. There are some deaf people who refuse to sign but will speak for themselves and/or communicate using text.

- Wheelchairs, mobility scooters, stair lifts and ramps were invented and provided for people who are mobility challenged.

- Prosthetics were created for people who were born without limbs, or lost limbs due to an accident or as a consequence of being a casualty of war or for medical reasons.

Did all these inventions or adaptations happen overnight? No!

I am sure that you can think of other technological aids that have been invented and used to improve a deaf or disabled person's quality of life. Some technological aids were invented for the intelligence industry and then adopted or adapted for the deaf and disabled communities in response to campaigns, human rights issues, or to promote equality.

Whatever the reason, the technology is there for you, and encourages the acceptance and celebration of diversity.

Whatever your diagnoses may have been, there is greatness in you waiting for an opportunity to emerge from within.

Patience is a virtue acknowledged when things are out of control. With patience and calmness the solution to a problem can be realised and appreciated.

CHAPTER 4

Be Calm

In the presence of God there is righteousness, peace and joy. With God on my side my disability can be enabling.

The aim of this chapter is to encourage you to remain calm because calmness is a sign of strength, not weakness.

"Do not be anxious about anything, but in every situation, by prayer and petition, with thanksgiving, present your requests to God. And the peace of God, which transcends all understanding, will guard your hearts and your minds in Christ Jesus." Philippians 4:6-7 (NIV)

I had to approach my fears and anxieties with calmness! How could this be possible from the perspective of being told that I was deaf?

I found it difficult to assess my situation; past, present and future. The past I knew well; the present was not nice, challenging and frightening. As for the future, what future? Yet I had to try to maintain an attitude of calmness, and I was amazed at how calm and at peace I was – even in the middle of a frustrating situation.

Then I realised that as a person who is deaf, one of the assurances that I need on this journey is the assurance that God is with me, by His presence. As a hearing person, like

David I knew that God was with me. As Psalm 51:11 says, "Do not take Your Holy Spirit from me" (NKJV). But I felt that I had to be like Moses and ask God for His presence. God didn't deny his request; instead the Lord replied: "My presence will go with you, and I will give you rest" (Exodus 33:14, NKJV).

It was reassuring to Moses to know that God would be with him. Moses understood that if he could just get God on his side then his disability would not be as restrictive as it would be otherwise. I had to start believing that too.

"For the Lord your God is living among you. He is a mighty saviour. He will take delight in you with gladness. With his love, he will calm all your fears. He will rejoice over you with joyful songs." Zephaniah 3:17 (NLT)

In the light of these Bible verses I started to believe that God is more than able to be a calming influence in whatever situation I find myself, irrespective of my disability.

Have you heard someone say to another, "Calm down, calm down"? The person saying "Calm down" recognises that the other is distraught, agitated and perhaps being irrational. Therefore the person is actually saying, "I know you have a problem; I know you have been hurt and probably disappointed, or I know you have received bad news, but let's take a deep breath, let's look at the situation from a different perspective, and you will be all right."

Calmness is a virtue we possess but have not taken time to cultivate. My faith and relationship with God was crucial to my circumstances, notwithstanding my doubts and fears. I realised that Philippians 4:6-7 was for me, from God.

When I was told that I had hearing loss, I lost all rationality pertaining to life. Fear and shame took over my life at that instant. These are very powerful emotions – I was a wreck.

You see, a person may appear calm when their environment is calm. However, a person's reaction to pressure, disappointment and chaos displays the truth about the person's emotion, and even their relationship with God. And if I may be so bold, it shows how real and tangible their faith is.

I went through several unbearable emotional torments, such as anger, which was never a part of me before. I was angry at God and people. I became easily irritated, especially when someone said something that I was unable to hear properly. I went through depression, and nobody understood what I was going through.

I also tried to avoid people as much as possible. There is a tendency for some people who are not 'disabled' to put deaf and disabled people down because they have a wrong perception of them. They don't see the person, only their disability. Consequently, out of ignorance or sympathy, they may be annoying. However, if you can maintain your 'calm' in such situations, you will experience God's presence. Do not be offended, defensive, bitter, angry or sarcastic. Defensiveness and negative emotions will not allow God's presence to be evident in your life; they tie you up in knots of bitterness, anger and a sense of inadequacy (low self-esteem and self-confidence).

The calmness I am talking about here is not indifference. There is a difference between true calmness and indifference, which is a coldness that may or may not provoke others. I am talking about a calm person who loves peace and displays the nature of God. The Bible says: "Blessed are the peacemakers, for they will be called children of God" (Matthew 5:9, NIV).

This peace is more than the absence of conflict, although that can be a part of it. It is the peace of God, the 'Shalom' of God, and it incorporates harmony, unity, security, patience and justice. Though we live in a world of violence, persecution, deceit and greed, God still wants His children to display this virtue of calmness and tranquillity in the face of opposition.

I wonder how your life has changed since your deafness or disability, especially the things you took for granted?

Recently the Lord drew my attention to birds singing. This was something I never took much notice of in the past. He was challenging me to stand still and to appreciate His creation. Since I was diagnosed with hearing loss I have had to wear hearing aids, so on this day, opening my window for fresh air, the first sound I heard was awesome. I was moved to tears with appreciation of God's goodness. Then this Bible verse popped up in my spirit:

> "Are not two sparrows sold for a penny? Yet not one of them will fall to the ground outside your Father's care. And even

the very hairs of your head are all numbered. So don't be afraid; you are worth more than many sparrows." Matthew 10:29-31 (NIV)

I have come to realise and conclude that my hearing loss did not surprise God: He allowed it, and He could have disallowed it. Perhaps you might not understand what I am saying here, so let me explain further.

Why did God create a sparrow that could be sold for a penny? My answer is for His pleasure.

Why is God's eye on a sparrow that could be sold for a penny? My answer is to protect it. So why is God's eye on me? My answer is to protect me, for I am more valuable than any sparrow.

Why is God's eye on a sparrow that could be sold for a penny? My answer is to provide for it. So why is God's eye on me? My answer is to ensure that I, His child, am not destitute.

Why is God's eye on a sparrow that could be sold for a penny? My answer is so that He could be glorified. So why did God allow me to become deaf? My answer is so that He may be glorified by me and through my continued belief, trust, faith, praise and dependency on Him.

"Therefore I tell you, do not worry about your life, what you will eat or drink; or about your body, what you will wear. Is not life more than food, and the body more than clothes? Look the birds of the air; they do not sow or reap or store away in barns, and yet your heavenly Father feeds them. Are you not much more valuable than they?" Matthew 6:25-26 (NIV)

Do you still doubt God's love for you because you are deaf or disabled? Stop! Cease from such thoughts, because the love of God for you is unfathomable. He proved it by giving His only Son, Jesus Christ, to redeem you and give you hope. It is a fact, whether you believe it or not.

As a sparrow sings regardless of the weather, I believe God wants us to praise and honour Him at all times. Through it all, learn to believe and lean on Jesus, learn to depend upon His Word. He will see you through.

Here is a short poem about being calm:

I know your ability

I know your disability

That is why I am your ability

Will you rely on Me?

I know your anxiety

I know your fear

That is why I say fear not

Will you trust Me?

I have seen your tears;

I have put them in a bottle

I know your heartaches

Will you try Me?

I know your sitting (I know your position)

I know your standing (I know where you are at)

That is why I offer to be with you.

I know my expectations

(My plans and purposes)

I know your limitations

Don't lean on your own understanding

Will you believe Me?

I know your longings

I know your expectations

That is why I say your expectations will not be cut off.

I know that you can't do anything without Me

That is why I AM your strength

I know you can't find your way without Me

That is why I AM the Way

I know you can't trust anyone because they let you down

I have not asked you to lean on man because the arms of flesh shall fail you

Look to me, the Author and Finisher of your faith

That is why I AM the Truth

Be still and know that I AM your Lord

I will be exalted above the heavens

That is why I AM the life,

I can be your life.

Is your anxiety, fear and despair because you feel lonely or alone? As a Christian, know and believe that God is with you and that He is in control; He has your world in His hands. He will not give you more than you can deal with. He will never leave you or forsake you, He said so. Believe and confess this: God does not lie.

"God is not a man, that He should lie, nor a son of man, that He should repent. Has He said, and will He not do? Or has He spoken, and will He not make it good?" Numbers 23:19 (NKJV)

"But seek first the kingdom of God and His righteousness, and all these things shall be added to you." Matthew 6:33 (NKJV)

Your disability is not the end of the world, though it may be the end of the way you used to do things. Now is the time to begin discovering new ways of doing things. It is an opportunity to look forward to a new future and new you.

"I have told you all this so that you may have peace in Me. Here on earth you will have many trials and sorrows. But take heart, because I have overcome the world." John 16:33 (NLT)

ACTION POINT

Desire the peace of God to guide you.

Jesus is the Way, the Truth and the Life.

Look beyond your disability, take control of your life and trust God.

Make a decision to move on to the next level.

CHAPTER 5

What is the Way Forward?

My aim in this section is to inform and encourage you that there is a way forward. Look to the hills (Calvary) from where your help comes from:

"I will lift up my eyes to the hills – from whence comes my help? My help comes from the Lord, Who made heaven and earth. He will not allow your foot to be moved; He who keeps you will not slumber. Behold, He who keeps Israel shall neither slumber nor sleep. The Lord is your keeper; the Lord is your shade at your right hand. The sun shall not strike you by day, nor the moon by night. The Lord shall preserve you from all evil; He shall preserve your soul. The Lord shall preserve your going out and your coming in from this time forth, and even for evermore." Psalm 121 (NKJV)

There is life and hope after a negative diagnosis. Our future depends on us taking the necessary small steps we need to start and continue on the journey of change.

"Trust in the Lord with all your heart; do not depend on your own understanding. Seek his will in all you do, and he will show you which path to take." Proverbs 3:5-6 (NLT)

This scripture has become real to me as I have sought to change.

Incidentally, we do live in a fallen world, that is, a world that is at variance with God's will and purpose. Consequently, your disability may not be a result of your sin or even the sins committed by your parents. In John 9:2-3, Jesus' disciples asked Him: "'Rabbi... why was this man born blind? Was it because of his own sins or his parents' sins?' 'It was not because of his sins or his parents' sins,' Jesus answered. 'This happened so the power of God could be seen in him.'"

People with certain limitations may be feeling that God is punishing them and they deserve what they are going through, because of sin in their life. Do not be deceived, the enemy, Satan the Devil, is a liar. If you have sinned and if what you are going through is a result of your sin, God is faithful and just: He will forgive you of your sin and cleanse you from all unrighteousness, when you go to Him, confess the sin and repent of it – i.e. stop and turn away from the sin.

Have you asked yourself what it means to trust in the Lord with all your heart and not to lean on your own understanding? In my desire for a miracle and healing for my hearing loss, I was told to trust in God and that He would do it. Well, I believe in God, I know He is able, but what do I do when I am unable to hear everything people are saying to me?

I was also told to have faith. I have faith in God, but I was suffering in silence. The questions I kept thinking when I was offered hearing aids were, "What's next? What is the way forward?" Then I thought, "I am trusting in God," so I refused to wear the hearing aids, believing God for a miracle.

Unfortunately, the enemy had influence over my emotions; I became angry at God and other people, as I felt that God was not honouring my faith in Him. People didn't understand the battle going on in my mind.

However, the above questions came to mind again and again: "What's next? What is the way forward?" I wasn't sure if I was living in denial or if I should just accept the hearing loss as being allowed by God and move on. It dawned on me that it was time to move on and accept any assistance being offered in order to fulfil God's purpose for my life.

I realised that trusting in God alone was not the only issue, but demonstrating my trust, moving in faith in order that His will be done in and through my life. Therefore, living out the trust that I had in Him was of more importance than my emotions. I am glad to say that God is still in control and that He will do what He needs to do in His own time, not mine, for He makes all things beautiful in His own time, not mine, hallelujah! Does it mean that I have stopped praying or believing in God? No! Not at all, as a matter of truth I will continue to praise Him, as a testament of my faith in His faithfulness, until my joy is full. Meanwhile, I have accepted His will as my will by accepting the assistance offered to me.

At this point, dear brothers and sisters, I need to ask, are you trusting God for your miracle of healing? The healing could be physiological, psychological and/or how you see yourself. Trust God with all your heart, do not lean on your own understanding and in all your ways acknowledge Him and He will direct your path. He is an all-wise God and He is able to do all things in His way and time, not yours; do not try to figure things out. Your responsibility is to acknowledge Him and allow Him to show you which path to take to receive the help He has prepared for you.

In order for us to exchange our disability for His ability, the reality of completely trusting in God whatever our circumstances can't be overemphasised. As we acknowledge our limitations and rely not on anything that we can do in our strength, but rather give all of the strength we have both physically and mentally to the Holy Spirit our helper, then we can say like the Apostle Paul that, in my weakness, God is my strength.

Now let's look at the story of Moses, when God called him to lead the Israelites out of Egypt.

God spoke to Moses from a burning bush. God told him what He wanted him to do, but Moses looked at his limitations, his inadequacies (including some sort of speech impediment) and presented this before the Lord. The Lord challenged Moses to trust him. He said to Moses:

"Who gave human beings their mouths? Who makes them deaf or mute? Who gives them sight or makes them blind? Is it not I, the Lord? Now go; I will help you speak and will teach you what to say." Exodus 4:11-12 (NIV)

When God commissioned Moses to free the Israelites in Egypt from Pharaoh, Moses could only see his inadequacies. What is the 'inadequacy' in your life that is holding you back from maximising your potential?

When I first discovered that I had hearing loss, my first thought was, "How can I carry on as a Sunday School teacher?" I needed to hear well. I decided I was going to strike a deal with the Lord. I said to God, "You need to heal me or I might have to step down from teaching your people." I have since come to some understanding of how God operates; we can never dictate to God and we can't box Him in. I have repented and moved on in my calling without looking back; in fact, I have started a Bible club ministry (Let's Talk About the Bible) where we meet to discuss the Bible. I no longer allow my limitation to limit what God wants to use me to do; rather, I have come to the realisation that I am just a tool in His hands and that He can use me as He deems fit to minister to His people. Therefore, all I need to do is to obey Him, just as Moses obeyed and saw the salvation of the Lord.

Despite his limitation, Moses was able to free the children of Israel from the stronghold of Pharaoh, with God's help. Do you know that the Bible nowhere says that God healed his speech impediment, but that didn't stop God from using him powerfully?

Where are you in the journey of life? Are you looking at what you don't have or are you looking at the God who is able to use what you do have? If you can only take your eyes off your limitations and look up to the God of limitlessness, then you will sing a new song because His power will be made manifest in your weakness.

I can hear God saying to you: "I will be with you and I will supply all your needs." He is totally sufficient, capable, adequate and faithful, so use what you have and God will supply what you don't have. In some cases, what you think you need, you really don't need. Who knows, if Moses had been a fluent spokesman it might have disqualified him from leading the Israelites out of Egypt? This is because the type of commission God gave him did not permit him to brag to or persuade Pharaoh; all he needed to do was to demonstrate the power of God and to tell Pharaoh what Jehovah, God, the All-Sufficient One, said.

God does not rely on your ability but your availability. He is waiting for you to exchange your disabilities for His ability. Sometimes people may look at you and make comments like Nathanael made about Jesus' place of birth:

"'Nazareth!' exclaimed Nathanael. 'Can anything good come from Nazareth?'" John 1:46 (NLT)

Is your disability linked to you being a single parent, your place of birth, your colour, your culture, your speech, your marital status, or your background (e.g. from a single parent home or an abusive home), etc?

If only you can believe that you have the great I AM residing inside of you and allow Him to manifest His grace and glory through you, then people will begin to see the glory of God in you. Then they will confess that indeed it can only be God at work in your life.

In some cases what looks like tragedy in your life God will use to turn your life around, and make you strong; that so-called 'disability' is an opportunity for God to show Himself – strong, loving and caring. Once again, what are you doing with your deafness or disability? Are you allowing it to put a limit on you and your future, or are you using it as a stepping stone to fulfil your dreams and God's plans for your life? Enough of the self-pity party!

I do not know where you are at this stage of your life, but have you allowed God to have His way in your life or are you still struggling to come to terms with your deafness or disability? I assure you once again that your help comes from the Lord, the Maker of heaven and earth. He loves you regardless of your limitations; this is the truth. God loves you the way you are.

People may have written you off, but be encouraged that God has not finished with you yet because the best is yet to come. Dear reader, will you allow God's power to be seen in you now as you exchange your disability for His ability?

What's next? Trust God and have faith in His Word. Receive strength to move forward. Whatever you do, don't allow the enemy of your soul to win the battle; take your questions, your discouragements and anxieties to God in prayer.

Give your burdens to the Lord, and He will take care of you. "He will not permit the godly to slip and fall" (Psalm 55:22, NLT).

The way forward is realising who you are and what you can do with what you have.

I say to you in the name of Jesus Christ of Nazareth:

"Arise, shine, for your light has come, and the glory of Lord rises upon you." Isaiah 60:1 (NIV)

CHAPTER 6

What Do You Have?

My aim in this section is to get you to think about and realise what you have.

You might say, "I have nothing, or only my leg, or an arm or an eye, or my child/children, or I have fear of tomorrow"... the list is endless.

Think again. It may seem insignificant to you; it could be a dream, an ability to draw, your ability to sign, a desire to do something, a talent, or even your deafness or disability. Whatever it may be, bring it to God and exchange it for His glory today.

Is your story similar to the woman Elisha met in the Bible (2 Kings 4:1-7)? A widow, she was afraid that she would lose her sons because of debts left by her husband. Her situation seemed hopeless, but God provided a way out:

"The wife of a man from the company of the prophets cried out to Elisha, 'Your servant my husband is dead, and you know that he revered the Lord. But now his creditor is coming to take my two boys as his slaves.' Elisha replied to her, 'How can I help you? Tell me, what do you have in your house?' 'Your servant has nothing there at all,' she said, "except a small jar of olive oil." 2 Kings 4:1-2 (NIV)

You see, Elisha demonstrated God's character. When he heard her fear, he asked, "How can I help you?" God is asking you today, how can He help you? Elisha said, "Tell me what you have in your house." If I were you I would quickly tell God what I have. Tell Him, say it. What you realise you have is what He will use to turn your situation around. In some cases, God has already provided a way out of the need that you want satisfied. God wants to use what you have to set you up for good.

Remember the story of Moses in the previous chapter? When God called Moses and told him to go to Pharaoh and tell him to let the Israelites go, Moses was terrified because of his inadequacies. God asked, "What is that in your hands?" Moses replied, "A rod." His shepherd's rod became the rod of God – a symbol of God's power. Even that was not enough for Moses! So God allowed Aaron his brother to go with him (see Exodus 4:14-17). But you do know something? Because Aaron was not part of God's original plan, he 'messed up', and so did his sons (much later in the book).

My question to you again is, "WHAT DO YOU HAVE?" You, personally; do you have hope, an attention to detail, limbs, mobility (even if you need to use a wheelchair, a mobility scooter or a walking frame), an ability to draw, think, reason, plan or create something good and positive? Do you have an ability to communicate (orally, or in writing, or with illustrations and/or by using sign language). You may think that what you have is small and insignificant, but what does that matter? You have something!

Notice I didn't ask, "WHO do you have?" The people in your life, whether family, friends, companions or carers, are temporary, not permanent. Some may even be a hindrance and not a help to your situation.

The widow said to Elisha, "Your servant has nothing there at all, except a small jar of olive oil." Praise God, at least she realised that she had a jar of oil. What do you have? The woman did not say, "My sons," because she thought she was about to lose them to slavery.

Do you know something? God doesn't want us to be inactive or negative, but actively thinking, working and depending on Him in every area of our life. Elisha's instruction amazes me. He said: "Go around and ask all your neighbours for empty jars" (2 Kings 4:3, NIV).

Why is Elisha instructing this woman to do this? She is depressed, frustrated, without hope and a lonely widow for that matter. Why on earth does Elisha want to embarrass her? Why doesn't he just give her the money to pay the debts and probably buy some bread for her children? I believe that could have been enough, a temporary solution, for the woman to at least save her children from slavery. But thankfully Elisha (through God) saw the bigger picture; he didn't want to sort her out temporarily, but provide A PERMANENT SOLUTION. He told her not just to collect one or two jars, but as many as she could. He said: "Don't ask for just a few" (verse 3).

He wanted her to use her faith, even in the presence of fear, because it takes faith and courage to go around to every neighbour and ask for empty jars. It takes faith to obey and boldness and courage to ask for more than one or two, thereby fulfilling the instruction. He continues by saying:

"Then go inside and shut the door behind you and your sons. Pour oil into all the jars, and as each is filled, put it to one side." 2 Kings 4:4 (NIV)

Without the knowledge of what God was going to do, this really doesn't make sense. She could have complained to Elisha, "Did you hear my story, what I said? I said I need money to pay my husband's creditors immediately, NOW! And I don't want to tell people my business. I don't want to hang my dirty laundry out for everyone to see. What has pouring oil got to do with money?!"

But this woman did not argue, she only obeyed. She did exactly as Elisha instructed her. In verses 5-7 of the same chapter (NIV) we read:

"… They brought the jars to her and she kept pouring. When all the jars were full, she said to her son, 'Bring me another one.' But he replied, 'There is not a jar left.' Then the oil stopped flowing. She went and told the man of God, and he said, 'Go, sell the oil and pay your debts. You and your sons can live on what is left.'"

Praise God! Following her obedience, faith and action, a miracle took place: A PERMANENT SOLUTION. Are you thinking, "Well, that is that woman. I have nothing"? Remember my story in the first chapter of this book, where I said that I had promised

God that I would write a book in honour of His name if He could heal me first? What a good bargain! No, because God is not going to submit to my terms and conditions. But in hindsight, using what I have – my hands, my eyes and intellect – to start writing this book, I have obeyed Him, first. I have put my faith in Him to act. I write the book and leave the rest to Him.

Dear reader, what do you have? Is it a rod, a jar of oil, an idea, a prayer, the will to live, pride, confidence, hope, or faith? Or are you still saying, "I have nothing except this one arm, one eye, deafness and/or an inability to speak, sign or move? Yes? Do you want to know what you can do with what you have? Then take a step of faith, know what you have and give it to God. God is the Lord of your yesterday, today and tomorrow. He can work with what you surrender completely to Him. In the book of Mark, Jesus worked a miracle with a few loaves and fish:

> "Taking the five loaves and the two fish and looking up to heaven, he gave thanks and broke the loaves. Then he gave them to his disciples to distribute to the people. He also divided the two fish among them all. They all ate and were satisfied, and the disciples picked up twelve basketful of broken pieces of bread and fish. The number of the men who had eaten was five thousand." Mark 6:41-44 (NIV)

What a miracle!

Imagine Jesus sitting down, thinking like His disciples, writing the names of everybody and giving them number tags to be sure that everybody got served. Afterwards, He would ask His disciples to distribute the loaves of bread and the fish to everyone. I can assure you that, while writing the names and numbers, He probably would have soon given up because He would have been discouraged, thinking that the loaves and fish would not be enough to feed the crowd.

But thank God, Jesus did not think like His disciples, or like us. Jesus saw a need and then He looked up to God the Father, the provider of all resources, and told Him what He needed by thanking Him. He thanked His Father for the provision with faith and confidence. His faith and confidence was based on the fact that the first miracle had happened – they had received some loaves and fish. He therefore believed for the rest of the miracle, instructing the disciples to distribute the food to everyone. His obedience was a demonstration of His faith, and His faith caused God to act on the words of His prayer and praise in order to provide another miracle!

What do you have? Give thanks to God in anticipation of His revelation of how to use what you have. Obey Him and take a step of faith. Give that part of your body that's causing you anxiety to Him today and you could see the glory of God revealed. A word of caution, though. God may not provide in the way, the place or at the time you want Him to. Remember the widow in 2 Kings 4, and finally God's words in Isaiah:

"'For my thoughts are not your thoughts, neither are your ways my ways,' declares the Lord. 'As the heavens are higher than the earth, so are my ways higher than your ways and my thoughts than your thoughts.'" Isaiah 55:8-9 (NIV)

God can take your minus and make it become a plus, but first we need to seek God and His righteousness in order to gain the ability to think differently.

ACTION POINTS

- Come to terms with your disability.
- Take stock of what you have left.
- Think of how to use it and take action.

TALK TO GOD

- Dear God, thank You for the gift of life.
- Please God, help my unbelief.
- Father, I totally surrender to You. Help me to use what You have given instead of looking for what I don't have.

CHAPTER 7

Change the Way You Think

"For as he thinks in his heart, so is he."
Proverbs 23:7 (NKJV)

My aim in this section is to enable you to realise and appreciate that your thoughts affect your attitude, behaviour, decisions, dreams and future. And what you think is influenced by what you see, watch, read and hear, including the company of friends you have.

Have you ever asked yourself, "What am I thinking?"

In my opinion this is an important question that each one us has to pause and ask ourselves from time to time. What is going on in your mind? I do ask it myself periodically, especially when I realise that my thinking is not in line with the Word of God. I sometimes say to myself, "If God were to put what you are thinking right now on a screen, Joy, would you be happy for everyone to see or read it?" I then quickly ask God for help to change my thinking, straightaway. Sometimes I try to justify my thinking, but who am I kidding? I am kidding myself, of course; as the saying goes, 'garbage in, garbage out'.

Dear reader, what do you think about your disability? What do you think about yourself? Are you thinking, "That is unfair", or are you trying to justify your negative thoughts? I urge you to stop and rethink, if you want to be all that God has intended you to be.

"Do not be confirmed to this world, but be transformed by the renewing of your mind, that you may prove what is that good and acceptable and perfect will of God." Romans 12:2 (NKJV)

There is a connection between our thoughts and what happens around us. The things you allow into your mind from what you read, the company you keep, what you watch, the things you see and what you listen to and hear regularly all eventually affect you. Therefore, you need to ask yourself, do these things build me up, or pull me down? Are they encouraging and positive or filling my mind with doubts and limitations? Does it influence my view of life positively or negatively?

Be careful of what goes into your mind because there is a great connection between your thoughts, your actions, and the outcome of your life. There is a need for you to take your focus off your deafness or disability, even your negative environment, and begin to see yourself as God sees you, because you are complete in Him. Don't give in to self-pity. People, including your family members and friends, may never know or understand what you are going through, but God does.

Maybe your disability or deafness was as a result of someone else's action, either intentionally or accidentally. Or you yourself may have been the cause of the disability or deafness, or you may have been born with it; whatever the cause, it is not something you should focus on right now, because it has happened. It has passed. It is in the past. What is more important right now is what you do with your life. God is calling you to come to Him with your disability, seek to know Him intimately and hear the peace He speaks to you, to your heart. Ask Him to give you the ability and wisdom to invest your time, talents and strength in knowing and serving Him and others. If you will stop focusing on your deafness or disability and instead desire to appreciate who you are, and seek to be a blessing to other people, God will do more for you, with you and through you than you can ever imagine.

You have a lot of worth, so do not allow anyone or anything to make you feel inferior. I have learnt that without my consent no one can put me down. I encourage you therefore not to allow anyone, or your deafness or your disability to make you feel inferior because you are special to God. Don't compare yourself with anyone else. You are unique!

God knows everything about you. He knows your pain, He sees your tears, and above all He loves you unconditionally. His love for you never changes.

It's amazing how God's words put things into the perspective of eternity, in order to remind us that our present life is temporary. On occasions we are reminded that, compared with eternity, the challenges we experience in the here and now, including living with our disabilities, are temporary. They are considered light and momentary afflictions with a prize to gain.

"Therefore we do not lose heart. Though outwardly we are wasting away, yet inwardly we are being renewed day by day. For our light and momentary troubles are achieving for us an eternal glory that far outweighs them all. So we fix our eyes not on what is seen, but on what is unseen, since what is seen is temporary, but what is unseen is eternal." 2 Corinthians 4:16-18 (NIV)

We are not to deny our disability or deafness but to focus on God's power in us. We are to be honest about our limitations and at the same time we are to see God's plan and power at work in our lives. We need to consider our situation and believe that in the long run we can and will achieve our purpose, which will bring glory to God. Paul did not lose heart, for he set his mind on the unseen glory to come; so we are being encouraged to look to that which is not seen.

What is your self-image like? In other words, how do you view yourself – positively or negatively? Have you developed a low self-image as a result of your deafness or disability? As you change your thought pattern you will be able to accept yourself just as you are. You need to acknowledge the fact that we all have strengths and weaknesses. If you have a positive self-image it does not mean that you are complete, it simply means that you have accepted what you can't change and are willing to change what you can, by being yourself and being happy with or accepting the way you are. If you can view your disability as just part of yourself and not a totality of your being, then you will develop a balanced concept of yourself and as a result your self-image and self-esteem will begin to improve.

Some deaf or disabled people place unnecessary pressure on themselves by trying to meet other peoples' standards. For example, in my own case as a hard-of- hearing person, I used to think that I couldn't do certain jobs that I was interested in because of my disability. But wait a minute, in hindsight, that was over-generalising, that was wrong thinking, because I can actually do so many other things. I have come to understand I just have to focus on my strengths and the opportunities that present themselves, not my weaknesses. You also are capable of doing a lot of things. Once again, change your thinking; don't pressurise yourself or compare yourself to others; don't let anyone or society shape your self-image.

The psalmist says:

"I praise you because I am fearfully and wonderfully made; your works are wonderful, I know that full well." Psalm 139:14 (NIV)

WOW! Unique, set apart, marvellous, individually made and not a duplicate, you are a masterpiece! That's awesome!

"For we are His workmanship, created in Christ Jesus for good works, which God prepared beforehand that we should walk in them." Ephesians 2:10 (NKJV)

"Finally, brothers and sisters, whatever is true, whatever is noble, whatever is right, whatever is pure, whatever is lovely, whatever is admirable – if anything is excellent or praiseworthy – think about such things." Philippians 4:8 (NIV).

The Apostle Paul encourages us to focus our thoughts on positive things, things that will lift us up.

I ask you: "What do you think about your disability? Is it true, noble, right, pure, lovely and admirable? Because only those things that are excellent and praiseworthy are worth thinking about. Therefore, you should not focus on bitterness, anger, offense, disappointment or unforgiveness."

ACTION POINT

- See the life of Jesus flowing through your disability as a way of producing abilities in other peoples' lives.
- Your limitation can't be compared to the eternal weight of glory.
- See God manifest His power in your weakness.
- Focus on the true Word of God concerning your situation.
- Seek out lovely things about others and yourself.
- Think on these things!

TALK TO GOD

- Dear Heavenly Father, thank You for my life.
- Help me to think on those things that will transform my life from negative to positive.
- I praise You, God, because I am unique

- Father God, help me to see myself the way that You see me.

CHAPTER 8

Forgiveness is the Way to Wholeness

"For if you forgive other people when they sin against you, your heavenly Father will also forgive you. But if you do not forgive others their sins, your Father will not forgive your sins." Matthew 6:14-15 (NIV)

In this chapter I want to show the importance of forgiveness. It is a requirement of a loving God who first forgave us our sins.

In the scriptures, Jesus made the importance of forgiveness clear because our Heavenly Father will not forgive us if we are unforgiving towards others. Therefore it is imperative that we do all that is within our ability to let go of grudges, seek restitution and avoid blaming others. If we do not, we end up with a broken relationship with God and others. Yes, it is difficult sometimes to forgive other people who have hurt us badly. But the truth is, if we do not forgive it will short-circuit our ability to live the Christian life the way God commands us to live it. It is therefore important for us to learn to forgive the way the Lord forgives us, so that we can enjoy true freedom, joy, peace and wholeness in our total being.

Forgiveness is a choice we make. What this means is that we can decide not to dwell on hurts, disappointments, injustice and negative behaviour and attitudes, and not to hold grudges against anyone who has hurt us deeply. The Bible says in the book of Hebrews:

"Their sins and lawless acts I will remember no more." Hebrews 10:17 (NIV)

I was in search of an appropriate definition of forgiveness that would fit into this chapter and I came across this:

"Forgiveness is a decision to let go of resentment and thoughts of revenge. The act that hurt or offended you might always remain a part of your life, but forgiveness can lessen its grip on you and help you focus on other, positive parts of your life. Forgiveness can even lead to feelings of understanding, empathy and compassion for the one who hurt you." From: http://www.mayoclinic.com/health/forgiveness/MH00131

Forgiveness doesn't mean that you deny that the person hurt you or their responsibility for hurting you, and it doesn't minimise or justify the wrong. You can forgive the person without excusing the act. Forgiveness brings a kind of peace that helps you to get on with life.

What attracted me to the definition was the fact that the writer listed the benefits of forgiving someone. It says that letting go of grudges and bitterness can make way for compassion, kindness and peace, and forgiveness can lead to:

- Healthier relationships
- Greater spiritual and psychological well-being
- Less anxiety, stress and hostility
- Lower blood pressure
- Fewer symptoms of depression
- Lower risk of alcohol and substance abuse

In my case I have learnt to forgive others by putting the words of Jesus into practice:

"Father, forgive them, for they do not know what they are doing." Luke 23:34 (NIV)

I paraphrase it in this way. I say:

"Joy, forgive them for they do not know what they are doing or saying or what they have done."

Why do I do that? Because I have realised that if I take every offence personally, or to heart and get offended, I will do more damage to myself than good. In any case, the people who use offensive words or laugh at my disability might be acting in ignorance, so why should I allow someone else's ignorance to hold me captive or in bondage? I have decided even before people offend me that I am going to forgive them for the sake of my own spiritual and physical wellbeing. This may not be an easy task initially, but through the help of the Holy Spirit it can be done.

For instance, if your deafness or disability was caused by someone else's negligence or mistake such as an accident, and to make matters worse the person refused to admit their fault, you need to forgive the person. Do not be angry, resentful or bitter, and do not allow the incident and your condition to dominate your life. It is far better to forgive than to live with a wounded spirit, because when you bring your pain and hurt to

God, He enables you to let go of your painful memories. With God, all things are possible!

The Mayo Clinic puts it this way:

"Forgiveness is a commitment to a process of change. To begin, you might:

- Consider the value of forgiveness and its importance in your life at a given time.

- Reflect on the facts of the situation, how you've reacted and how this combination has affected your life, health and well-being.

- When you're ready, actively choose to forgive the person who's offended you.

- Move away from your role as victim and release the control and power the offending person and situation have had in your life."

This is what the Word of God says:

"And whenever you stand praying, if you have anything against anyone, forgive him and let it drop (leave it, let it go), in order that your Father Who is in heaven may also forgive you your [own] failings and shortcomings and let them drop."
Mark 11:25 (AMP)

God knows how difficult it is to forgive. I believe that He is offering to help us, if we are willing and take the first step to forgive.

Do not underestimate what the devil can do in the area of unforgiveness. I know that he will give you a catalogue of reasons why you should hold a grudge, be bitter and remain bitter, or desire revenge. The devil knows that if you do not forgive your offender then he has a right to control your decisions and your life. As a result of this knowledge, I have made a consistent effort to forgive and ask God daily to examine my heart and help me to live daily in forgiveness. The devil is subtle and he wants you to justify every reason why you should not forgive, but remember that unforgiveness will hurt you much more than the person you refuse to forgive. So for your own sake, forgive and let go. Don't say, "I can't forgive", do not be deceived by the devil; you can forgive and you must forgive. Don't go by your feelings; deliberately, purposely be determined to forgive.

I must bring to your attention that everyone – with or without deafness or disability – will at some point in their life be hurt and offended. As a deaf or disabled person some people may dislike you, perhaps they may think that you are a burden, but remind them that they need you as much as you need them, and you have something to offer humanity and society.

Finally, in spite of how people might treat us, Jesus said we must forgive. Let us remind ourselves of the ending of the Lord's Prayer:

"For if you forgive other people when they sin against you, your heavenly Father will also forgive you. But if you do not forgive others their sins, your Father will not forgive your sins." Matthew 6:14-15 (NIV)

Let's ask Him to help us to forgive all those that have hurt or betrayed us.

Confess the sin of unforgiveness daily and forgive. But if you struggle to forgive, then ask God to help you to forgive every day of your life. Use prayer and praise as a weapon against the devil and his schemes and traps of unforgiveness.

The reward for forgiving others is great, it is liberating!

ACTION POINTS

- Believe God for a miracle
- For the sake of your health, forgive
- For your spiritual well-being, forgive

TALK TO GOD

- Father, help me to forgive all those who have hurt me
- Father, I bring my pain and disappointment to you
- Father, help me to move on as I forgive myself and others who have sinned against me

CHAPTER 9

Confessing Your Way Out of Disabling and Limiting Thoughts With God's Enabling and Empowering Promises

The aim of this chapter is to introduce you to the act of confessing God's promise as often as you need to. It should become your daily medication. You can never overdose on it, but it can empower you and enable you to realise and release the potency of God's Word in and through your life.

It is written:

"Therefore, I urge you, brother and sisters, in view of God's mercy, to offer your bodies as a living sacrifice, holy and pleasing to God – this is your true and proper worship. Do not conform to the pattern of this world, but be transformed by the renewing of your mind. Then you will be able to test and approve what God's will is – his good, pleasing and perfect will." Romans 12:1-2 (NIV).

Therefore, I refuse to conform to the pattern of this world. Rather I will renew my mind with the Word of God daily, so that I can know and do His will.

It is written;

"Therefore, strengthen your feeble arms and weak knees. 'Make level paths for your feet,' so that the lame may not be disabled, but rather healed." Hebrews 12:12-13 (NIV)

Therefore, I receive strength in my feeble arms and weak knees and I exchange my disability for God's ability.

It is written:

"If you listen carefully to the LORD your God and do what is right in his eyes, if you pay attention to his commands and keep all his decrees, I will not bring on you any of the diseases I brought on the Egyptians, for I am the Lord, who heals you." Exodus 15:26 (NIV)

Therefore, if I listen to the Lord and obey Him completely, none of the diseases of the Egyptians shall come near me.

It is written:

"Praise the LORD, my soul; all my inmost being, praise his holy name. Praise the LORD, my soul, and forget not all his benefits – who forgives all your sins and heals all your diseases, who redeems your life from the pit and crowns you with love and compassion, who satisfies your desires with good things so that your youth is renewed like the eagle's." Psalm 103:1-5 (NIV).

Therefore, I praise the Lord with my total being for all the benefits He bestows upon me, most especially for forgiving me of all my sins and healing me of all my disabilities, for I am crowned with love and compassion.

It is written:

"Then they cried to the LORD in their trouble, and he saved them from their distress. He sent out his word and healed them; he rescued them from the grave. Let them give thanks to the LORD for his unfailing love and his wonderful deeds for mankind." Psalm 107:19-21 (NIV).

Therefore, I cried to the Lord in my trouble and he saved me from my distress, His Word healed me and He delivered me from the grave, so I will give praise to the Lord for His love for me.

It is written:

"He gives strength to the weary and increases the power of the weak. Even youths grow tired and weary, and young men stumble and fall; but those who hope in the LORD will renew their strength. They will soar on wings like eagles; they will run and not grow weary, they will walk and not be faint." Isaiah 40:29-31 (NIV)

Therefore, I am not tired, I am not weak or weary, for the Lord renews my strength and I will soar on wings like eagles.

It is written:

"Surely He has borne our griefs (sicknesses, weaknesses, and distresses) and carried our sorrows and pains [of punishment], yet we [ignorantly] considered Him stricken, smitten, and afflicted by God [as if with leprosy]. But He was wounded for our transgressions, He was bruised for our guilt and iniquities; the chastisement [needful to obtain] peace and well-being for us was upon Him, and with the stripes [that wounded] Him we are healed and made whole." Isaiah 53:4-5 (AMP)

Therefore, since Jesus Christ has borne my grief, my sorrows and pains, and I am not ignorant of the price that Jesus paid to bring me healing and peace, I boldly declare that I am whole, well and there is nothing broken and nothing missing in my body.

It is written:

"But I will restore you to health and heal your wounds,' declares the LORD, 'because you are called an outcast, Zion for whom no one cares." Jeremiah 30:17 (NIV)

Therefore, I declare my wounds are healed and my health restored.

It is written:

"Beat your ploughshares into swords and your pruning hooks into spears. Let the weakling say, 'I am strong!'" Joel 3:10 (NIV)

Therefore, I believe and confess that I am strong.

It is written:

"But for you who revere my name, the sun of righteousness will rise with healing in its rays. And you will go out and frolic like well-fed calves." Malachi 4:2 (NIV)

Therefore, I revere the name of God and declare that the sun of righteousness is rising upon me with healing, and I am whole.

It is written:

"'If you can?' said Jesus. 'Everything is possible for one who believes.'" Mark 9:23 (NIV)

Therefore, I believe. I have no doubt in my mind about the power of Jesus and everything is possible to me because I believe.

It is written:

"Therefore I tell you, whatever you ask for in prayer, believe that you have received it, and it will be yours." Mark 11:24 (NIV)

Therefore, I believe that I have received my healing because I have asked in prayer.

It is written:

".... they will place their hands people who are ill, and they will get well." Mark 16:18 (NIV)

Therefore, I lay my hands on myself now and I receive my healing in Jesus' name.

It is written:

"... I have come that they may have life, and have it to the full." John 10:10 (NIV)

Therefore, I receive abundant life in Christ Jesus. I refuse any lesser life in any area of my life.

It is written:

"... how God anointed Jesus of Nazareth with the Holy Spirit and power, and how he went around doing good and healing all who were under the power of the devil, because God was with him." Acts 10:38 (NIV)

Therefore, I believe through the power of the Holy Spirit that was on Jesus Christ that I am healed, delivered and made whole.

It is written:

"Christ redeemed us from the curse of the law by becoming a curse for us..." Galatians 3:13 (NIV)

Therefore I believe and confess that I am redeemed from every form of curse.

It is written:

"... being confident of this, that he who began a good work in you will carry it on to completion until the day of Christ Jesus." Philippians 1:6 (NIV)

Therefore, I have confidence that Christ will complete the good work that he has started in me.

It is written:

"'He himself bore our sins' in his body on the cross, so that we might die to sins and live for righteousness; 'by his wounds you have been healed.'" 1 Peter 2:24 (NIV)

Therefore, I believe and confess that I have been healed because Jesus Christ paid the price for my sins, and I now die to sin and live a righteous life.

It is written:

"Dear friend, I hope all is well with you and that you are as healthy in body as you are strong in spirit." 3 John 1:2 (NLT)

Therefore, I believe all is well with me in my body and my soul prospers.

It is written:

"And they have defeated him [Satan] by the blood of the Lamb and by their testimony. And they did not love their lives so much that they were afraid to die." Revelation 12:11 (NLT).

Therefore, I believe and confess that I have defeated the devil by the blood of the Lamb and I am victorious in every area of my life, in Jesus' mighty name.

Thank you, Jesus, for I am joyful and have peace all the days of my life. AMEN.

Confessing God's Word is a way of knowing who you are and what you have in Christ, in order to live free of the devil's devices and develop a 'zoe' (full) life.

CHAPTER 10

Use What You Have

The aim of this chapter is to remind you of what you have and how to use it. By realising what you have, you can release and use it with confidence, conviction and wisdom.

The Lord asked Moses, "What is that in your hand?" (Exodus 4:2, NLT). When God commissioned Moses to free the Israelites from the hold of Pharaoh, Moses could only see his inadequacies. There was something that Moses had but had not realised its significance. God had to help him to see the significance of his rod or shepherd's staff. The rod represented power and authority! What do you have that you can use to release and maximise your potential?

When I first discovered that I had hearing loss, my first reaction was, "I am a Senior Benefits Officer, how can I carry on with my job, with all those meetings and telephone work? How will I cope? What do I do? Do I give up my job?" Also, as a Sunday School teacher, "How will I teach, interact and control the group? I need to hear well."

At the time I didn't realise that my ability to hear God spiritually was more important than physical hearing, which can be interrupted or distorted by other noises. I wonder if this is what Paul the Apostle went through when he talks about the 'thorn' in his flesh, and how he asked God three times to remove it and

God's response was, "My grace is sufficient for you, for my power is made perfect in weakness" (2 Corinthians 12:9, NIV).

Like the Apostle Paul, Moses and other people God used in the Bible, such as Deborah, Joseph, Daniel and Esther, to name a few, God wants our availability. This is the demonstration of our desire to serve, worship, adore and obey Him: a simple, child-like faith and dependency on an Almighty and Awesome God. Don't doubt that God Jehovah, the All-Sufficient One, is waiting for you to realise what you have and desire to know how to use it.

I can hear God encouraging you to take that step of faith, do something you haven't dared to do before, because of your previous negative, depressive and limiting thinking. He is totally sufficient, complete and able to use what you have. And in some cases, what you don't have, you don't need.

The Apostle Paul had a thorn in his side, but God used him nonetheless.

Sometimes people may look at you and make comments like Nathanael did about Jesus' place of birth:

> "'Nazareth!' exclaimed Nathanael. 'Can anything good come from Nazareth?'" John 1:46 (NLT)

If only you can believe that you have the great I AM residing inside of you and allow Him to manifest His grace and glory through you, then people will begin to see the glory of God in you. Then they will confess that indeed it can only be God at work in your life.

In some cases what looks like tragedy in your life is what God uses to show you the inner strength that you have, and to even give you a different perspective on life, as well as the wisdom to release your latent skills and abilities. Once again, what are you doing with your deafness or disability? Are you allowing it to put a limit on you or are you using it as a stepping stone to fulfil God's plan for your life?

Your limitation may be the comfort of your bed, your 'comfort zone'. Your bed may not be physical but mental. Your negative self-pitying: the "I am a victim", "Nobody loves me", "Nobody cares about me", "Why should I bother?" way of thinking.

Enough of the self-pity party! I say to you, in the name of Jesus Christ of Nazareth, take up your bed and walk!

Do you have the ability to think good, energising thoughts? Do you have the ability to dream big dreams with small beginnings? Do you have the ability to plan, to communicate, to smile and laugh? Do you have determination? Do you have access to the Internet? Is there someone around you who is blocking your progress? Are you in a disabling environment? If you have access to the Internet it can help you to find support and assistance from somewhere else. There are people local to you who can help you.

If you have the determination to make something of your life, then use what you have, no matter how small or insignificant it may seem. Use it! Like the widow in 2 Kings 4, like Moses in Exodus, and like Jesus when He fed the five thousand.

If you know Christ, you will know life. Reach out to God right now and He will reach out to you and raise you up, because YOU are the most important asset in your life!

"Arise, shine, for your light has come, and the glory of the LORD rises upon you." Isaiah 60:1 (NIV)

We are told that:

"The weapons of our warfare are not carnal but mighty in God for pulling down strongholds…' 2 Corinthians 10:4 (NKJV)

Continue with your daily confessions and be obedient to the Word of God. Understand and apply His Word and promises to your circumstances and you will start to develop coping strategies that will help you to overcome the limitations that surround your life.

CHAPTER 11

Developing Strategies For Coping With Your Deafness or Disability

In this chapter the aim is to enable you to realise and accept that you are not a victim, you are victorious.

"Yet in all these things we are more than conquerors through Him who loved us." Romans 8:37 (NKJV)

I have heard people say that having something and losing it is worse than not having it at all.

This means that people may behave differently with regards to their disability depending on how they became deaf and/or disabled. A person who became deaf or disabled in the course of their life, through an accident or because of an illness, may behave differently from someone who was born deaf or disabled. Some may be resigned to their circumstance, while others may be angry and bitter and expend their energy blaming others, while others could be depressed, withdrawn and lose the will to live.

For instance, in my own case, I was born hearing and then I became deaf. I was told it would be a miracle for me to hear well again; that was not good news to me. It took a toll on my emotions and brought on frustration, confusion, embarrassment, fear and anger, because I would have to tell people about my deafness. As a result, I decided that avoidance was a better option.

It is natural that you will go through stages of grief, denial, anger, depression and the 'why me?' stage. But also at some point try to figure out how the disability may affect other things in your life. I have dealt with issues of loss and emotions in my first book **'Help My Heart'.** You can refer to this book if you want to know more about how to handle loss and grief.

Some of the important strategies for coping with your deafness or disability are:

- Talk about it. Let others know about your deafness or disability, especially if it is not visible.

- Seek help. You may need support and advice from other people, support groups and professionals.

- Be careful – watch what you allow yourself to hear and accept about your deafness or disability.

- Do not focus on your deafness or disability – because you will be thinking of and seeing their limiting effects on your life.

- Stay positive. Do not stay at a support group or listen to a person who focuses mainly on the limitations or negative aspect(s) of your deafness or disability.

- Keep your temper. If people are rude, ignorant or patronising in their behaviour towards you, ignore them or make an excuse and move away from them. Hold your breath, and count to 10 or 20. Do not take their comments personally or to heart. Do not get angry and do not respond when you are angry.

- Keep socialising. Do not allow anyone or anything to cause you to isolate yourself from others, because you may do yourself more harm than good.

- Meditate on God's Word and focus on the future.

- Try new things – see what else you can do and achieve.

- Try new ways of doing things. Maybe you were right-handed and have lost the use of your right hand. Why not practise using your left hand? At first it will be frustrating, but think long term – think of the joy you will feel when you see your achievements.

- Be happy with every achievement, no matter how small or insignificant it may seem.

- Reassure yourself daily. Tell yourself that you can do what you have set your mind to do, because God's Word says: "I can do all things through Christ who strengthens me" (Philippians 4:13, NKJV).

It is important to know that you can be healed emotionally, even if the physical disability or deafness is noticeable.

You need to come to terms with your deafness or disability, accept it and move on. Of course, this may take time, but I can tell you with confidence that with the help of the Holy Spirit and my family I have found a reason to live again, so you can too! They reminded me of who I am in Christ. This is very important – as we will see in the next chapter.

CHAPTER 12

Who Are You?

The aim of this chapter is to encourage you to know who you are without restrictions, bias or prejudgement (prejudice).

Jesus knew who He was: the Son of God and the Son of man. He was confident in who He was. But He knew that other people were not sure who of His identity, so He asked His disciples in the Gospel of Mark:

"'Who do people say I am?' They replied, 'Some say John the Baptist; others say Elijah; and still others, one of the prophets.' 'But what about you?' he asked. 'Who do you say I am?' Peter answered, 'You are the Messiah.'" Mark 8:27-30 (NIV)

Jesus was confident in who He was. No one could take away this knowledge. He knew His purpose in life and no one could distract Him from His mission. He was in the world but not of the world. He was unique, special, an original. He was the God-man.

Expectations of yourself and other people's expectations of you

If I were to ask those who know you, "Who you are?" what do you think their response would be? You may not be who others say you are, or be able to do what they expect you to do, or do things in the way they may expect you to do things. You may not speak or behave in the way they expect you to. That does not mean that you are any less a person. You are a person who does things in your own unique and special way!

"... you do not belong to the world, but I have chosen you out of the world." John 15:19 (NIV)

Like Christ, you are in the world, but God does not expect you to conform to the things and ways of the world. He does not want you to be a clone or a duplicate of another person, whether it be your mother, father, brother, sister, best friend, aunt, uncle, famous person, etc. God expects you to be an original individual because He has a specific and original plan and purpose for your life.

You need to know that you are valued by God and that He cares for you. When you accept this fact you can be assured that there is a purpose in your situation, and finding that purpose should be your focus.

You also need to accept the fact that others might not have confidence in you. People may discriminate against you directly or indirectly, or distance themselves from you. You need to accept this as common practice and do not take it personally or allow it to affect you in a negative way. You can actually turn the tide around by using the disability as a stepping stone to acknowledge that the people that discriminate against you and other deaf or disabled people are simply ignorant about the subject. If only they knew your worth, they would change their attitude towards you. Your chance meeting or employment might turn out to be the link that connects them to their destiny. You actually have something to offer.

RECLAIM YOUR DREAM and REALISE YOUR POTENTIAL.

If your deafness or disability has caused you to lose focus, it is time to recapture your destiny. If you focus on what you don't have you will lose sight of what you do have, and you will eventually see only your disability instead of realising and releasing your latent talent or ability. If your goal is to serve God then trust God to help you; He will supply what is missing in your life and challenge you to aim high.

Loving yourself just as you are

In Mark 12:31 (NIV) Jesus says that the second most important commandment, after loving God, is: "Love your neighbour as yourself."

You know God wants you to love others, but He also wants you to love yourself. However, if you have been in an environment where the love given is dependent on performance, I want to let you know that God's love is not like that. He loves us unconditionally. It is clear that God loves you and me without any reservation.

"I have loved you with an everlasting love..." Jeremiah 31:3 (NIV)

You need to love yourself. The main 'hurdle' in some people's lives is their inability to love themselves.

Since God created you, you do not have to base your love on someone else's approval or try to meet other people's expectations of you. God's love for you is so great that even if you do not know God or have a relationship with Him, His word says that He loves you:

"For God so loved the world that he gave his one and only Son, that whosoever believes in him shall not perish but have eternal live". John 3:16 (NIV)

If you can meditate on this verse you will not need anyone to tell you how to love yourself. So, decide to love yourself, take care of you; but ensure it does not result in self-centeredness, arrogance, pride or unbridled ego. You are special to God so do not allow anyone not even yourself to put you down. Act as a redeemed, saved and loved child of God. On the other hand, if you have not yet received Christ into your life or given your life to Him, you are not 'saved' and you cannot fully understand the love of God because you are not part of God's family. I urge you to go to the back of this book and pray the salvation prayer.

The Bible tells us to love our neighbour as we love ourselves:

"You shall love your neighbour as yourself." Mark 12:31 NIV.

There is no way you can love your neighbour as yourself without a spiritual transformation; also you cannot love yourself as you ought to without the saving knowledge of God, through Jesus Christ; therefore salvation is crucial.

Your confidence and identity

Where is your confidence and identity? Is it in things or people? Is it in your past achievement? Jesus says:

"For where your treasure is, there your heart will be also." Matthew 6:21 (NIV)

Whatever (or whomever) your confidence and identity is in, that is what you have given the right to control you. Your past, people and circumstances can hold you back from your future and control your destiny by making you weak and weary. Eventually you will lose focus and the desire for change or to achieve.

"For you have been my hope, Sovereign LORD, my confidence since my youth." Psalm 71:5 (NIV)

In your seemingly hopeless situation, God's command to you is to be hopeful. Whatever happens, never give up your hope for a better tomorrow because life without hope is not worth living.

Be hopeful, I say again, be hopeful! For example, if you were sure that by tomorrow all your needs would be met, would you still be downcast? I guess your answer is 'no'. So take courage in the sovereign Lord and let Him be your confidence, for He has never failed and He will not fail you. He is too faithful to fail you. In order to have confidence, you must have unshakeable hope and faith in God.

"But we have this treasure in jars of clay to show that this all-surpassing power is from God and not from us." 2 Corinthians 4:7 (NIV)

Who is this treasure spoken about? It is the very nature of God. God Himself finds you worthy to dwell in – you – by His Spirit! He has chosen to live in you, an empty jar of clay (your body). Wow! As for me, I am happy to know that the creator of the whole universe resides in me. What other assurance do you and I need? Nothing more than that.

In my opinion, deafness, disability and ability are all irrelevant when we give our all to the Sovereign Lord. When we give God His rightful place in our lives, we can do the seemingly impossible and overcome the challenges we face from time to time. We can be transformed day by day. Praise God! Let your confidence be in the Lord.

Your lack of confidence could be as a result of many factors, including internal factors such as feelings of inadequacy, lack of self-esteem or shame. Or it could be external factors such as fear of what people will say, fear of the unknown or fear of failure. Whatever has caused your lack of confidence can be brought to the Lord in prayer. Trust Him, because He has promised that He will be with us. Without a doubt, this should give you the confidence to move on.

Even when the deafness or disability seems to be an obstacle, see it as an opportunity for God to display His greatness and then your confidence will soar.

> "But now, this is what the Lord says – he who created you, Jacob, he who formed you, Israel: 'Do not fear, for I have redeemed you; I have summoned you by name; you are mine. When you pass through the waters, I will be with you; and when you pass through the rivers, they will not sweep over you. When you walk through the fire, you will not be burned; the flames will not set you ablaze. For I am the Lord your God, the Holy One of Israel, your Saviour; I give Egypt for your ransom, Cush and Seba in your stead. Since you are precious and honoured in my sight, and because I love you, I will give people in exchange for you, nations in exchange for your life." Isaiah 43:1-4 (NIV)

Wow, this scripture blows my mind! God loves me – He knows my name – I am precious to God. Not only that, I am honoured in His sight; He will even go to the extent of giving others for my life. If I were you I would meditate on this scripture until it sinks into every fibre of your being, because even if nobody else cares for you the God of the whole universe is passionate about you!

If you can base your confidence on this it will enable you to walk tall, regardless of what you have and what you do not have.

God has made you important to others. They need you whether they realise it or not.

> "And the eye is not able to say to the hand, I have no need of you, nor again the head to the feet, I have no need of you. But instead, there is [absolute] necessity for the parts of the body that are considered the more weak.

And those [parts] of the body which we consider rather ignoble are [the very parts] which we invest with additional honour, and our unseemly parts and those unsuitable for exposure are treated with seemliness (modesty and decorum), which our more presentable parts do not require. But God has so adjusted (mingled, harmonised, and subtly proportioned the parts of) the whole body, giving the greater honour and richer endowment to the inferior parts which lack [apparent importance], so that there should be no division or discord or lack of adaptation [of the parts of the body to each other], but the members all alike should have a mutual interest in and care for one another. And if one member suffers, all the parts [share] the suffering; if one member is honoured, all the members [share in] the enjoyment of it. Now you [collectively] are Christ's body and [individually] you are members of it, each part severally and distinct [each with his own place and function]." 1 Corinthians 12:21-27 (AMP)

Who are you?

Only you can answer this question. Who do you say you are? To help you decide, I have listed some of the things that God says you are.

Who does God say you are?

You are the light of the world – Matthew 5:14

You are the salt of the earth – Matthew 5:13

You are a child of God – John 1:12

You are accepted – Ephesians 1:6

You are complete in Christ – 2 Corinthians 5:17

You are a jewel in His crown – Zechariah 9:16

You are the apple of His eye – Deuteronomy 32:10

You are adopted – Ephesians 1:4-5

You are safe and secure – Romans 8:1

You are beloved – Colossians 3:12

You are forgiven – Hebrews 9:14

You are free to be you – 1 Corinthians 15:10

CHAPTER 13

Believe and Develop a Winning Attitude

The aim of this chapter is to help you use your knowledge of who you are to believe in who you are, and develop a winning attitude.

In the previous chapter you read about who you are in Christ. I hope you appreciate that, irrespective of your physical or mental ability or agility, you and I are of equal value and worth to God. When God created the universe and mankind He was showing off His prowess, and He created something beautiful to rejoice in and with. God wants us to love Him first, then we can love each other.

"You are worthy, O Lord our God, to receive glory and honour and power. For you created all things, and they exist because you created what you pleased." Revelation 4:11 (NLT)

Are you a deaf or disabled person? You are capable of showing the beauty of God within you. Believe in who God says you are and let that inspire and motivate you into developing a positive attitude about yourself and your life.

In order to develop a winning attitude you need to train your mind to think positive thoughts, because your attitude determines your altitude in life. That is, your attitude can make you or break you, and it determines how far you will go in life.

Your state of mind is more important than your physical fitness. Do you know that you can practise every day in order to change the way you think? You can lose your negativity through the healthy and positive thoughts you have imbibed over the weeks, months and years you have been deaf or disabled.

It is essential to have a positive mental attitude to cope with your deafness or disability. When others fail to recognise your worth, do not take it to heart. Do not dwell on other people's insults or negative comments or patronising behaviour towards you; simply be yourself. And learn to laugh at yourself; this will help you to deflect and defuse the power and effect of insults and negative comments. Developing this skill will help you to win friends and influence people. Do not look for negativism, racism, sexism or discrimination in people's comments, because you will always find them! Much better to chalk it up to their ignorance and naivety and shrug it off like water off a duck's back.

The Bible calls developing a more positive and healthy way of thinking "renewing your mind" (Romans 12:2, NIV). This is more effective if you use God's promises.

For example, when you are deaf or disabled people are quick to tell you, "You can't do that." But God says we can do all things through Christ who strengthens us – see Philippians 4:13.

It may be true that you cannot do something the way other people do it, but nothing says you cannot try to do the same thing in a different way. A deaf person may need an interpreter or a speech-to-text typist in order to participate in a meeting. Or a disabled person may not be able to attend a meeting personally, for whatever reason, but now with video conferencing what is to stop them from participating in the meeting?

To be a winner requires more than a desire to win. You must develop a winning attitude by accepting your deafness or disability. Think of it as an opportunity to serve God and others in a different and unique way. Take advantage of any training opportunities that may be available as a way of personal development. Join support groups in order to network, keep up to date with technological, legislative and other changes, research and find ways of moving forward in life rather than wallowing in self-pity.

Brothers and sisters, I do not consider myself as an expert, however, one thing I do is:

> "Forgetting what is behind and straining towards what is ahead, I press on towards the goal to win the prize for which God has called me heavenwards in Christ Jesus." Philippians 3:13-14 (NIV)

I have discovered that the purpose of our existence is not about us but rather about God Himself. So, do not fear what will happen to you in the future because God has everything figured out, even before you were born.

CHAPTER 14

Hope Against Hope

What is 'hope'?

The Concise Oxford Dictionary defines it as:

"Noun – a feeling of expectation and desire; a cause or source of expectancy or grounds for expecting something to happen.

"Verb – expect and desire e.g. hoping for an offer of a job; intend, if possible, to do something."

Faith believes you will get what you're hoping for, even if you haven't seen it yet. Hope is not wishful thinking without any foundation, but is a confident expectation based on certainty.

As a Christian, hope consists of fully relying on God's promises, believing that what He has said will come to pass.

One of the key features of hope is time. When we hope, we are looking towards the future with an open heart about something we long for.

Abraham and Sarah had long passed the age of child-bearing and rearing when God gave them a promise. Contrary to the facts or possibilities, God had spoken and Abraham believed in the word of hope and had hope:

> "... who, contrary to hope, in hope believed, so that he became the father of many nations, according to what was spoken, 'So shall your descendants be.' And not being weak in faith, he did not consider his own body, already dead (since he was about a hundred years old), and the deadness of Sarah's womb. He did not waver at the promise of God through unbelief, but was strengthened in faith, giving glory to God..."
> Romans 4:18-20 (NKJV)

Supernatural hope is that which comes as a result of God's Word. God's Word fills your heart with the right ingredients. enabling you to wait, with faith. This enabled Abraham to see beyond human possibility. The hope of becoming a father of many nations, according to God's promise to him, was not taken lightly; it was mixed with faith.

Abraham and Sarah were quite old; Sarah had probably crossed the menopause decades before (Genesis 18:11). It seemed like a hopeless situation, with all the available evidence against their hope. But God changed all that.

How to start having hope as a person with disability

In the story of Abraham we've just looked at, the hope of ever having a child in the human sense did not appear normal. However, because he believed God, Abraham's desire was granted – though he had to wait.

Waiting is another issue when you have to hope for something that has not happened yet. You can become so anxious that you start looking for alternative ways of fulfilling your desire. Abraham did precisely that, and later it caused him heartache.

My view as a person with a disability is that hoping in God is not a passive act, it is very active. You need to believe and put your faith to work by meditating on the Word of God, as this is the basis of your hope.

Abraham believed and hoped in something that everyone could see was impossible. But God said it and therefore it came to pass, irrespective of the circumstance.

Perhaps you have lost hope entirely about life, success or livelihood. A word from God will change your situation for your good, but you have to search for it and be ready to accept it.

God's Word plants, waters and harvests hope in us. God watches over His Word to perform it, and His Word is forever settled in heaven. He has also promised that our hope will not be cut off.

The Bible says that Abraham "...not being weak in faith, he did not consider his own body, already dead (since he was about a hundred years old), and the deadness of Sarah's womb. He did not waver at the promise of God through unbelief, but was strengthened in faith, giving glory to God, and being fully convinced that what He had promised He was also able to perform. And therefore 'it was accounted to him for righteousness'" (Romans 4:19-22, NKJV).

This is a remarkable passage. We should change our focus from the reasons why it is impossible to do things to the reasons why and how it is possible to do things.

When we allow unbelief into our lives, we begin to stagger and stumble in our faith, and lose trust in the promises of God. This leads to double-mindedness and an unstable heart, which makes it difficult to hope and believe for the impossible.

An unstable heart and mind cannot hold forth hope. However, if you go back to the source of hope – God's Word – you will remain eternally strong, holding on until your hope is realised.

God is able to do exceedingly, abundantly, "immeasurably more than all we ask or imagine, according to his power that is at work within us" (Ephesians 2:20, NIV). Remember, God is not like a man, and He says His ways are not our ways (Isaiah 55:8), therefore, while we might be expecting Him to provide in one way, He might decide to do it another way.

For example, God has healed me emotionally and He is perfecting me physically. Sometimes healing might be progressive and sometimes it is instantaneous. Whatever way, we need to believe He knows the best for us and He will do the best for us. Be hopeful!

"And hope does not put to shame, because God's love has been poured out into our hearts through the Holy Spirit, who has been given to us." Romans 5:5 (NIV)

So far we have looked at hope and being hopeful, but what does to 'hope against hope' really mean? This phrase means to keenly want or desire something, even when the odds against getting it or achieving it are enormous. It is about clinging to a mere possibility.

It is derived from the Bible, where Paul describes Abraham as one who, "against all hope, believed in hope, that he might become the father of many nations, according to that which had been spoken" (Romans 4:18, NIV).

This phrase in itself seems to encourage hope every time it is used.

Sometimes, you may ask yourself if something or someone is worth it, hoping against hope that it is or they are. Yes, it is worth it, if your hope is anchored on the creator of heaven and earth.

Let's look at the story of Simon Peter's obedience in Luke 5:

> "He [Jesus] got into one of the boats, the one belonging to Simon, and asked him to put out a little from the shore. Then he sat down and taught the people from the boat. When he had finished speaking, he said to Simon, 'Put out into deep water, and let down the nets for a catch.' Simon answered, 'Master, we've worked hard all night and haven't caught anything. But because you say so, I will let down the nets.' When they had done so, they caught such a large number of fish that their nets began to break. So they signalled to their partners in the other boat to come and help them, and they came and filled

both boats so full that they began to sink." Luke 5:3-7 (NIV)

Peter was in the pit of hopelessness, having exhausted all his wisdom, business expertise and strength without having anything to show for it. He was already calling it quits when the Master of the universe stepped in and told him to hope for a catch of fish from the same water that had been unproductive all night. One lesson from this is that God uses obedience to meet the needs of His children.

Jesus said, "'Put out into deep water, and let down the nets for a catch.' Simon answered, 'Master, we've worked hard all night and haven't caught anything. But because you say so, I will let down the nets.'" (Luke 5:4-5, NIV).

The Lord asked him to make another effort in the same lake; and Peter reluctantly, nevertheless, hope against hope, obeyed. His obedience yielded fantastic results.

We could also look at the story of Joseph in Genesis. His hope started with a dream (Genesis 37:5). From then on, it was hope against hope that he depended on. God had spoken. The dream was not fulfilled until a long time later (Genesis 41:44), but it happened.

When some people meet with difficulties in a particular business, they abandon it for another. This may not necessarily be the best thing to do. Even when it appears hopeless, just look to God. Use the word He shows you for that situation and enquire of the Lord how to use the word, obey it and wait for the result. To solve a particular problem or challenge, it is not necessarily the number of attempts made that matters, but who is aiding your attempts.

Peter had tried so many times without a catch that night, but the first and only attempt he made that had the backing of the Lord delivered to him a harvest beyond expectations.

The major challenge believers going through the path of hopelessness experience is that, unlike Peter, they lack the word from God regarding their situation. When there is nothing from God on an issue, the state of hopelessness will be worse. But if God has spoken a word on the matter, the case is as good as closed in your favour. Are you in a hopeless situation? Take time to read and study the Bible, and ask God to give you a word for that situation. God always has something to say about your situation, but are you ready to hear it?

During the writing of this book I got this title 'Hope against hope' and the following morning, as I was having my morning devotion, I used a devotional book called 'Open Heavens'. And guess what? The title of the devotion for that day, 2nd May 2012, was 'Be Hopeful' by Pastor E.A Adeboye. Citing the following two passages, Pastor Adeboye pointed out that God commands us to be hopeful in the midst of hopelessness:

"Happy is he who has the God of Jacob for his help, Whose hope is in the LORD his God..." Psalm 146:5 (NKJV)

"Wherefore, if God so clothe the grass of the field, which to day is, and to morrow is cast into the oven, shall he not much more clothe you, O ye of little faith?" Matthew 6:30 (KJV)

KEY POINT

Whatever happens, never give up your hope for a better tomorrow, because life without hope leads to hopelessness, despair and defeat.

Remember that "faith is the substance of things hoped for, the evidence of things not seen" (Hebrews 11:1, NKJV).

CHAPTER 15

Move On – Let Go and Let God

No, dear brothers and sisters, I have not achieved it, but I focus on this one thing: knowing the will of God for my life and obeying Him.

I did not take the news of my hearing loss well. I went through several unbearable emotional torments such as rejection, bitterness, jealousy, envy and anger – which was never a part of me before. I was angry at God and with people. I became easily irritated, especially when someone said something that I was unable to hear properly. I went through depression, and nobody understood what I was going through. I also tried to avoid people as often as I could.

However, God has enabled me to see things differently. I am no longer held back by my inability to hear well, but rather I have concluded that God has a reason for it, and I now have confidence that today He will take all the glory as He will not share His glory with anyone. I have also come to the conclusion that God still loves me, just as I am, and I love Him for who He is. I have decided to move on with the help of my family, friends, my faith in God and the working of the Holy Spirit in me. The Holy Spirit guarantees my inheritance (Ephesians 1:14) and He is my comforter and encourager, so I surrender to Him. Not my will, but His will be done at all times.

The secrets of letting go and letting God are:

- Know who you are from God's perspective.

- Know and accept what you can't do.

- Don't complain about the things you can't do.

- Leave what you can't do and get on with what you can do.

- Decide to make a difference with your life.

- Find out what God has to say about your situation, and obey and trust Him.

I have discovered that the purpose of our existence is not about us but rather about God Himself.

Recently I heard the voice of God saying to me, "What do you want? Your hearing or Me?" In response I said, "Lord, all I want is You. You are my priority – nothing else will do." Does that mean that I have given up on believing God for a miracle? No! Not at all. I still pray, believe and hope, but it is no longer my focus; what matters most is that I have God. So I have decided to let go of anger, irritation, depression, rejection, bitterness, jealousy and envy. Every day I give them to God.

I may not know the extent of your pain, your discouragement or distress, but God is aware of your situation and He will see you through.

Dear sisters and brothers, I encourage you to move on too. You may not know when your miracle will happen, but in the meantime enjoy each day, as it is a gift from God (the present!), and don't allow depression into your life.

I believe God knows the level of challenges each one of His children is able to bear, and so would not allow more than we can bear to come upon us. He is our burden-bearer, so lean on Him. Remember to hope against hope, move on and access the blessing of God through obedience.

ACTION POINT

- Grieve for your loss, no matter the disability, whether visible or invisible.
- Believe God still loves you and allow Him to wipe away your tears.
- Hand over your disability to Him and take on His ability.
- Make a decision to move on to the next level.

Finally, talk to God and say:

- Dear Heavenly Father, thank You for Your immeasurable love for me.
- You love me as I am, and, based on Your love for me, help me to see myself as You see me. Help me to love and accept myself as I am, for I am fearfully and wonderfully made by You.
- Father, I hand over my disability to You and I take on Your ability.
- Father, I believe I can do all things through Jesus who gives me power. Amen.

CHAPTER 16

What's Next?

I have exchanged my disability for God's ability.

I am free to be me in Christ.

What about you?

This is Lord Ashley of Stoke's story:

Lord Ashley of Stoke, the country's first deaf MP and "the greatest champion Britain's disabled have had", died aged 89. As a Labour MP, Jack Ashley represented the city of Stoke-on-Trent for 26 years and then was made a peer in 1992. Born in Widnes, Cheshire, Ashley was elected an MP in 1966 after working as a BBC journalist. Two years later he lost his hearing following an ear operation, and said in his autobiography that the last voice he heard was the late rugby commentator Eddie Waring.

A crash course in lip reading and the support of colleagues gave him the confidence to carry on his career in the House of Commons, after initially suggesting he wished to resign his seat.

In a sign of the respect in which he was held, MPs, including political foes such as Prime Minister Edward Heath, turned towards him during Commons debates so that he could get a clear view of their mouths to lip read. "Early on, when I first lost my hearing, I think people were a little fearful about attacking me," he said. "But as I re-established my confidence, that soon fell away."

BBC presenter Andrew Marr said that during his career the peer had won important victories "for victims of the drug thalidomide, for victims of army bullying and for victims of domestic violence."

Dame Ann Begg described Ashley as "a trailblazer who made it possible for me to even think I could be an MP." Gordon Brown said, "Jack Ashley was the greatest champion Britain's disabled have had. He was compassionate, direct, forceful and radical. The man spoke with the authority of personal experience and took the cause of disabled men and women into the chambers of Parliament and to the heart of government.

"He leaves behind a contribution in legislation and policy progress for the cause of tackling disability that will not easily be surpassed."

I do hope this brief story encourages and inspires you to make your challenges stepping stones to greatness. The greatness may only be recognised by your family and friends, maybe your community and work colleagues. It doesn't matter; what is important is that you have changed and you are living and writing your own story for your future.

I leave you with this message:

> "Do not be anxious about anything, but in every situation, by prayer and petition, with thanksgiving, present your

requests to God. And the peace of God, which transcends all understanding, will guard your hearts and your minds in Christ Jesus.' Philippians 4:6-7 (NIV)

"I have told you these things, so that in me you may have peace. In this world you will have trouble. But take heart! I have overcome the world." John 16:33 (NIV)

The rest is now **your** story!

FREEDOM PRAYER

John 8:36 (NIV) says that "if the Son sets you free, you will be free indeed."

In order to be free indeed you need to accept Jesus Christ into your life.

Say this prayer:

> Heavenly Father, I come to you in the name of the Lord Jesus Christ. I am sorry for my sins. I ask Your forgiveness. Thank You for dying on the cross for me, to set me free from my sins. Please come into my life and fill me with your Holy Spirit and be with me for ever. Thank You, Lord Jesus. Amen.

If you have sincerely prayed this prayer, then you are born again and you are free from slavery to sins, bondages and limitations. I congratulate you!

CHAPTER 17

Deaf Awareness

SEE THE PERSON, ANTICIPATE THEIR POTENTIAL.

DON'T FOCUS ON THEIR DEAFNESS.

Many people are daunted at the prospect of communicating with a deaf person. Many think that having a pen and paper is the best solution, but it's not always.

Some think communicating with a deaf person means using British Sign Language (BSL); again, not always.

A large number of deaf people use these methods of communication but they're not the only way to converse with a deaf person.

It is best to be aware of this, and be prepared with a few different techniques which can be used to remove barriers that prevent deaf people from communicating effectively.

The UK Council on Deafness points out that nearly 15 per cent of the UK population – that's nine million people – is deaf or hard of hearing, including 30,000 children under the age of 16. But still many deaf people are denied access to their GP surgery, restaurants, place of worship, shops, government offices and hospitals. For instance, research shows that nearly 70 per cent of people who use British Sign language as their first language have asked for an interpreter to be booked for a GP appointment, but did not get one.

Many people and employers are often unaware or confused about how best to reach those who are deaf. And many employers are reluctant to employ deaf people.

TIPS ON HOW TO INTERACT WITH PEOPLE WHO ARE DEAF OR A LINGUISTIC MINORITY PERSON

- Remember that each person is unique.
- Don't think you know what they need.
- Let the person show you how they prefer to communicate.
- It is wrong to assume that a deaf person wearing hearing aids can hear what is being said. The person may only be able to hear specific frequencies of sound or background noise.
- Don't assume that all deaf people wear hearing aids. Many deaf people do not wear them. That is why deafness is referred to as the hidden or invisible disability.

How can you know if a person is deaf?

The ability to identify a deaf person can be difficult but here are some clues:

- The way they speak may be different.
- The deaf person may speak louder than others because they can't hear themselves speak.

- Pronunciation of words may be different or not clear. E.g. the deaf person may say they have 'fish' when they mean they have 'finished'.
- You may enter a room and the volume on the TV or radio is very high, or a person may request that the volume on a TV or radio is turned up high.
- A person may request repetition of what has been said.
- If a person stares at your face it may be an indication that they are trying to read your lips in order to know what you are saying.

How can I get their attention?

- Don't shout.
- Don't stand behind the person.
- Get eye contact; this is very important.
- You can tap the deaf person gently on their shoulder or on their arm.
- To get a deaf person's attention from a distance: wave, stamp your feet on a wooden floor, or use flashing lights.
- When you enter a room, flick the light switch on and off so that the deaf person knows that someone else is in the room.

How do I communicate with a deaf person?

- Let the deaf person show you. If the person asks a question using their voice, it is safe to assume that they will be expecting to lip read your reply.

- Some rules of lip reading:
    - Face the person.
    - Keep eye contact.
    - Speak clearly, at a normal pace.
    - Do not shout.
    - Ensure there are no bright lights behind you that could make it difficult to see your face.
    - Use whole sentences, not one word replies – using sentences gives contextual clues.
    - Minimise background noise, such as radio or TV, or visual noise such as moving wall displays in classrooms.
    - Use facial expressions to help explain – for example back up directions by pointing.
    - If there is more than one person speaking, take turns to talk: do not speak over the other person.
- Don't patronise the deaf person.
- Don't underestimate their potential.

Lip reading is not easy – in fact, it's 70 per cent guesswork – so:

- Help give visual clues through your facial expressions.
- Don't jump from one topic to another.
- Establish the context when you speak.

- Speak clearly; don't obstruct your lips with sweets, knife, fork, spoon, cigarette or moustache.
- Don't keep repeating yourself – you are not a parrot. If the deaf person does not understand something you said, try to find a different way of saying it, or tracking back and explaining the context. Use appropriate examples, and, if required, draw, write and or use role play.
- If you're not managing to express yourself, don't give up – try something else. Perhaps you could text your message on your mobile phone, write it down on a piece of paper, point to your subject, or even use hand gestures.
- Remember to: 'Repeat, re-phrase, and /or write it down.'

Just ask

If you are unsure about anything to do with a deaf person, ask the person. A deaf person would prefer to be asked about their level of deafness and how best to communicate, rather than be ignored out of some misguided sense that you may cause offence or confusion. This includes deaf children as well as adults: a child may lack confidence, and all the more so if they struggle to understand you. So don't give up or back off: just ask.

At Work

Some key things to consider in the workplace:

- Does your place of work have an induction loop? It needs to be checked regularly. Is it in the reception area and/or the deaf person's work area?
- The organisation should offer a range of contact options – not only a phone number.
- Ensure you have good signage to direct people where to go.
- In meetings, ask the deaf person where the best place is for them to sit
- Know where to hire a BSL interpreter if needed – see NRCPD (National Registers of Communication Professionals working with Deaf and Deafblind People) website.
- Consider BSL training for staff – contact Signature, links on their website or check other websites such as RAD (Royal Association for Deaf People), BDA (British Deaf Association), Remark!, Deafworks, Action on Hearing Loss (formerly RNID), to name a few.
- Seek advice and assistance from the Department for Work and Pensions, Access to Work department, with regards to assessing the needs of the deaf person and implementing the necessary changes and adaptations.

CHAPTER 18

Church Attitudes Towards Deafness and Disability

Do miracles still happen? Oh yes, I can confirm that "Jesus Christ is the same yesterday and today and for ever", according to Hebrews 13:8. If Jesus healed in the past, He still heals today and He will heal in the future.

What then are the explanations to give to those who are not instantly healed or made whole? Is there anything wrong with their faith? No. We might not have all the answers, but that does not mean to say the Word of God is ineffective.

How then do we handle someone who appears to have a seemingly permanent physical disability, and has not been healed after much prayer?

We do not have the answer to why some people are not completely healed. What we do know is that suffering came into the world as a result of the fall of mankind, though this statement is no comfort to anyone who is suffering.

Jesus had compassion for people with disabilities. In fact, He gives them special attention and promises them the sure hope of the resurrection and the transformation of their bodies. We should all follow His example.

The Bible teaches that God heals and so many instances in the New Testament confirm that Jesus performed miracles.

However, the Apostle Paul said this in the book of 2 Corinthians:

> "Therefore, in order to keep me from becoming conceited, I was given a thorn in my flesh, a messenger of Satan, to torment me. Three times I pleaded with the Lord to take it away from me. But he said to me, 'My grace is sufficient for you, for my power is made perfect in weakness.' Therefore I will boast all the more gladly about my weaknesses, so that Christ's power may rest on me." 2 Corinthians 12:7-9 (NIV)

The nature of the Apostle Paul's infirmity is not the issue of discussion in this book, but what I want to get across is the fact that the Lord gave Paul an unexpected answer to what he asked for. We can take heart in knowing that God's ways are not our ways and His thoughts are not our thoughts, because He is the only one who knows the end from the beginning. For that reason, He allows only the best in our lives, whatever it may be. Although we may not see the situation as being for our good or benefit in the short term, in the long run we will realise that "in all things God works for the good of those who love him" (Romans 8:28, NIV).

WHY ARE PEOPLE WITH DISABILITIES BEING TREATED DIFFERENTLY?

No one likes to admit to treating disabled people as inferior or second class, yet the way people behave at times gives out this message.

The following may be reasons why this happens:

- Ignorance: if you have never suffered a disability you may simply not understand exactly what people with disabilities face in life.

- Fear of embarrassment: can affect how we treat a disabled person. It is easier and perhaps less embarrassing to talk over the head of a deaf person to their 'able' friend than to make the effort, or even display your own discomfort, by trying to communicate directly with the deaf person. Our failure to do this, however, can be very humiliating to the person with a hearing loss.

- Ignorance of the Word of God: due to this, some people believe that mental and physical disabilities are punishments from God, or even the result of an evil spirit, and the disabled person is mistreated.

- Lack of compassion: Jesus had compassion for people with disabilities. In fact, He gives them special attention by reaching out to heal them. For example, in Matthew 8:2-3, "A man with leprosy came and knelt before him and said, 'Lord, if you are willing, you can make me clean.' Jesus reached out his hand and touched the man. 'I am willing,' he said. 'Be clean!' Immediately he was cleansed of his leprosy" (NIV). We should follow Jesus' example.

HOW CAN THE CHURCH SHOW ITS APPRECIATION OF PEOPLE WITH DISABILITIES?

The church needs to know and understand that each individual is important and loved by God.

Every person is significant and has a contribution to make to others in the world.

In ministering to people with disabilities, we are reminded of our own vulnerability as human beings. People with disabilities also remind us of the high value of human life and the unique contribution every person brings to the body of Christ.

The book of Deuteronomy says:

> "There will always be poor people in the land. Therefore I command you to be open-handed towards your fellow Israelites who are poor and needy in your land." Deuteronomy 15:11 (NIV)

The Bible teaches that every member of the body of Christ is valuable and worthy of honour, just as every part of our physical body has a special purpose. According to 1 Corinthians:

> "If one part suffers, every part suffers with it; if one part is honoured, every part rejoices with it." 1 Corinthians 12:26 (NIV)

People with disabilities are an integral part of the body of Christ and belong in our churches.

Our Christian faith gives direction for our attitudes and responses to people. The same principles apply to people with disabilities and to those relating to them.

HOW CAN WE MEET THE NEEDS OF PEOPLE WITH DISABILITIES IN OUR CHURCHES?

Jesus taught His disciples how to treat people with disabilities:

> "Then Jesus said to his host, 'When you give a luncheon or dinner, do not invite your friends, your brothers or sisters, your relatives, or your rich neighbours; if you do, they may invite you back and so you will be repaid. But when you give a banquet, invite the poor, the crippled, the lame, the blind, and you will be blessed. Although they cannot repay you, you will be repaid at the resurrection of the righteous.'" Luke 14:12-14 (NIV)

We are to make a special effort to reach those with disabilities. In the Old Testament we are given warnings about our attitude towards disabled people. The Lord will surely bless those who show kindness to people with disabilities:

> "Do not curse the deaf or put a stumbling-block in front of the blind, but fear your God. I am the LORD." Leviticus 19:14 (NIV)

We do not have the answer to why some people suffer more than others. However, as already mentioned, we do know that suffering came into the world as a result of the fall of mankind.

In my opinion the church can meet the needs of people with disabilities in the following ways:

- When pastors and ministers visit a patient whose injury from an accident has resulted in a permanent disability, they should reassure the patient that life still has purpose and value, even after the loss of a physical or mental ability. Church leaders can also help families and carers cope with the changes and challenges brought on by a loved one's recent disability and help them feel a sense of belonging in the body of Christ.
- The church needs to create a welcoming environment for people with disabilities, as well as their families and carers.
- The church that teaches that children born with special needs are valuable members of society must be ready to provide care within the church programmes for these children.
- The church needs to provide British Sign Language interpretation in services as a means of meeting the needs of the hard of hearing, deaf and deafened sign language users. Alternatively, a text-to-speech typist could be provided for deaf, deafened and hard of hearing people who do use sign language.
- The church has to make its venues accessible for people with disabilities. Research into the appropriate adaptations needs to be made and implemented.
- Those serving in churches need to be trained to be aware of the needs of deaf/disabled people. This

includes the way and manner in which they are approached, being polite, non-judgemental, welcoming, and promoting equal opportunities for all.
- There must be adequate support given to carers of people with disabilities within the church family.
- Encourage church members, if they so desire, to learn sign language or any other skill that will enhance the work of the church in the community.
- Provide deaf awareness and/or disability awareness training days.
- Provide signed and/or subtitled DVDs of sermons.
- Enable deaf and disabled people to participate in the events and programmes of the church by providing the necessary tools, equipment or personnel.

It does not matter what size the church is, what is important is that the church ministers to deaf/disabled people. This would communicate that a church is outward looking, meeting its objective of providing support in the local community.

CHAPTER 19

Some of the World's Famous People Who Are Deaf or Disabled

- **Pete Townshend** (Peter Dennis Blandford Townshend, born May 19, 1945 in Chiswick, London) – an award-winning English rock guitarist, singer, songwriter, composer and writer. A member of the famous rock band 'The Who', Townshend is losing his hearing and fears the disability will end his song writing career. He is blasé about hearing loss from a lifetime spent using headphones, but an expert says today's iPod generation is storing up trouble for the future by listening to music at high volumes.

- **Helen Keller** (Helen Adams Keller, June 27, 1880 – June 1, 1968) – an American author, activist and lecturer. She was the first deaf/blind person to graduate from college. She was not born blind and deaf; it was not until 19 months of age that she came down with an illness described by a doctor at the time as "acute congestion of the stomach" but which could have possibly been scarlet fever or meningitis. The illness did not last for a particularly long time, but it left her deaf and blind. Keller went on to become a world-famous speaker and author. She is remembered as an advocate for people with disabilities and numerous other causes.

- **Thomas Edison** (Thomas Alva Edison, February 11, 1847 – October 18, 1931) – an American inventor of Dutch origin and businessman who developed many devices that greatly influenced life around the world, including the phonograph and a long lasting light bulb. In school, the young Edison's mind often wandered. He was noted to be terrible at mathematics, unable to focus, and had difficulty with words and speech. This ended Edison's three months of official schooling. The cause of Edison's deafness has been attributed to a bout of scarlet fever during childhood and recurring untreated middle ear infections.

- **Geri Jewell** (born September 13, 1956 in Buffalo, New York) – an actress and comedian born with cerebral palsy. Jewell is most famous for her roles on the television programme 'The Facts of Life' and HBO's 'Deadwood'. Jewell brings to her presentations personal experience of having her behaviour and actions misunderstood because of her cerebral palsy. She is said to be a pioneer for comedians with disabilities.

- **Albert Einstein** (March 14, 1879 – April 18, 1955) – one of the most important great minds of his century. Einstein is known to have suffered from dyslexia, mainly because of his bad memory, which was shown by his constant failure to memorise the simplest of things. He could not remember the months in the year, yet he would succeed in solving some of the most complicated mathematical formulas of the time without any trouble. He may have never learned how to properly tie his shoelaces, but his scientific contributions and theories still have a major effect on all of today's current knowledge of science.

- **Stevie Wonder** (Steveland Hardaway Judkins, born May 13, 1950; his name was later changed to Steveland Hardaway Morris) – an American singer-songwriter, multi-instrumentalist and record producer. Blind from infancy, Wonder signed up with Motown Records at age twelve, a pre-adolescent age, and continues to perform and record for the label to this day. It is thought that he received excessive oxygen in his incubator which led to retinopathy of prematurity, a destructive ocular disorder affecting the retina, characterised by abnormal growth of blood vessels and sometimes retinal detachment.

- **Charles Dickens** (Charles John Huffam Dickens, FRSA, February 17, 1812 – June 9, 1870) – the foremost English novelist of the Victorian era, as well as a vigorous social campaigner. Dickens had the pen-name 'Boz', and is the author of such classic books as 'A Christmas Carol' and 'Oliver Twist'. He had epilepsy, as did several of the characters in his books. The medical accuracy of Dickens's descriptions of epilepsy has amazed the doctors who read him today. Through some characters in his novels, Dickens recorded observations on the nature of epileptic seizures, their causes and provocation, and their consequences. Three of his main characters, Monks, Guster and Bradley Headstone, had seizures which Dickens realistically described. (Source: Disabled World – disability news for all the family:
http://www.disabled-world.com/artman/publish/epilepsy-famous.shtml)

- **Richard Burton** (November 10, 1925 – August 5, 1984) – at one time the highest paid actor in Hollywood, Burton was well known for his

distinctive voice. He suffered from epilepsy all his life and slipped extremely deep into alcoholism to try to prevent the seizures. Eventually this led him to manic depression (now known as bipolar disorder) but he would never go to see a doctor because he did not trust them one bit. At times he seemed to be more scared of being crazy than having epilepsy. Throughout his life he never went to a doctor to be diagnosed. (Source: Disabled World –
http://www.disabled-world.com/artman/publish/epilepsy-famous.shtml)

- **Sir Walter Scott** (August 15, 1771 – September 21, 1832) – a prolific Scottish historical novelist and poet, popular throughout Europe during his time. Scott survived a childhood bout of polio in 1773 that left him lame. In 1778 Scott returned to Edinburgh for private education to prepare him for school, he was now well able to walk and explore the city and the surrounding countryside. His reading included chivalric romances, poems, and history and travel books. (Source: Disabled World –www.disabled-world.com)

- **F. D. Roosevelt** (Franklin Delano Roosevelt, January 30, 1882 – April 12, 1945) – the 32nd

President of the United States of America who played a big role during World War II. It was said that Roosevelt had several disabilities, including vision impairment. He was also the only President to ever get elected four terms in a row. This was due to the fact that his policies and strategies helped the economy to recover from recession. Roosevelt also aided the poor and unemployed of America and restored order at various times during his Presidency. (Source: Disabled World – www.disabled-world.com)

- **Christopher Reeve** (Christopher D'Olier Reeve, September 25, 1952 – October 10, 2004) – an American actor, director, producer and writer. He portrayed Superman/Clark Kent in four films from 1978 to 1987. In the 1980s he also starred in other films, including 'Somewhere in Time' (1980), 'Deathtrap' (1982), 'The Bostonians' (1984) and 'Street Smart' (1987). In 1995, Reeve was paralysed in an accident during an equestrian competition. He was confined to a wheelchair for the rest of his life. He lobbied on behalf of people with spinal cord injuries, and for human embryonic stem cell research, after this accident. He founded the Christopher Reeve Foundation and co-founded the Reeve-Irvine Research Centre. Reeve died at age 52 on October 10, 2004 from cardiac arrest caused by a systemic infection. (Source: Disabled World – www.disabled-world.com)

- **Louis Braille** (January 4, 1809 – January 6, 1852) – the inventor of Braille. Louis Braille became blind after he accidentally stabbed himself in the eye with his father's awl. He later became an inventor and designed Braille writing, which enables blind people to read through feeling a series of organised bumps representing letters. This concept has been beneficial to all blind people around the world and is commonly used even today. If it were not for Louis Braille's blindness he may not have invented this method of reading, and no other blind person could have enjoyed a story or been able to comprehend important paperwork. For more details see the RNIB website – http://www.rnib.org.uk/aboutus/aboutsightloss/famous/Pages/louisbraille.aspx

- **David Blunkett** (born June 6, 1947) – a British Labour Party politician, MP for Sheffield Brightside and Hillsborough and former Home Secretary. Blunkett was born with a genetic disorder that affected his optic nerve, rendering him completely blind. His family from South Yorkshire were very poor and disadvantaged, and his father died following an industrial accident in 1959. The already underprivileged family became even more destitute, and Blunkett seemed destined to be unsuccessful. He tried to gain enrolment at a school for the blind in Worcester, but he failed his assessment and was refused entry.

He eventually made it into the Royal National College for the Blind and then the University of Sheffield where he received his degree in political theory. It was difficult for Blunkett to make it as far as he did – his nature was to rebel and he completely disliked public school systems – but making it to university was a monumental step in his life. That rebellious streak may have, in fact, been his driving force that made him believe he was good enough to attend college and graduate despite his blindness. From graduation on, working his way up in the political system became easier and easier. Blunkett's story helps prove that if you have a goal, whether you're disabled or not, no one can fault you for your impairments if you show them they don't matter.

Blunkett said that being born with a disability can make everything in life more complicated. The person born with a disability may feel normal – since it is all he or she knows – but it quickly becomes clear that to succeed and have a life one would consider normal, you have to go through a number of tribulations. Of course, it is very possible for people with disabilities to go on and do great things. That journey can just be more arduous that it would be for others. The story of David Blunkett is a story of overcoming one's disability and flourishing against all odds. (Ref: The Political Sight of the Blind David Blunkett.)

- **Joni Eareckson Tada** (born October 15, 1949) – an evangelical Christian author, radio host, and founder of Joni and Friends, an organisation "accelerating Christian ministry in the disability community". As a teenager, Joni loved life. She enjoyed riding horses and loved to swim. One summer in 1967, that changed. While swimming with some friends, Joni dove into a lake not knowing how shallow it really was. She broke her neck, paralysing her body from the neck down. For the next two years during her rehabilitation, Joni struggled with her paralysis, with life and with God. Since then, Joni has learned to accept her disability, has written 14 books, recorded several musical albums, become an advocate for disabled people and an internationally known mouth artist. Joni says her personal relationship with God has helped her overcome the obstacles in her life, and she tells how you can experience the love of God, despite pain and suffering.

See http://www.jonieareck sontadastory.com

- **Walt Disney** (Walter Elias Disney, December 5, 1901 – December 15, 1966) – an American film producer, director, screenwriter, voice actor, animator, entrepreneur and philanthropist. Disney is notable as one of the most influential and innovative figures in the field of entertainment during the 20th century. He had dyslexia, which is a learning disorder characterised by reading difficulties. While Disney was attending high school he also went to the Academy of Fine Arts. This caused him to have double the school work of an average student, on top of the fact that he also dealt with being dyslexic. (Source: Disabled World –

- http://www.disabled-world.com/artman/publish/article_2130.shtml)

- **Richard Branson** (Sir Richard Charles Nicholas Branson, born July 18, 1950) – an English entrepreneur, best known for his Virgin brand of over 360 companies. Richard Branson has been involved in a number of world record-breaking attempts since 1985, when in the spirit of the Blue Riband he attempted to cross the Atlantic Ocean in the fastest recorded time. Branson has dyslexia, resulting in poor academic performance. He was the captain of football, rugby union and cricket teams, and by the age of 15 he had started two ventures that eventually failed, one growing Christmas trees and another raising budgerigars. But that didn't stop him becoming one of Britain's leading businessmen. (Source: Disabled World – http://www.disabled-world.com/artman/publish/article_2130.shtml)

- **Ludwig Van Beethoven** (December 16, 1770 – March 26, 1827) – German composer and pianist. Beethoven is a great source of confidence for disabled people, as he was able to create and play music even after going completely deaf – which of itself is quite a miracle. Beethoven conquered his disability and became one of the greatest musicians of all time. If there was one thing that affected his struggle to succeed it was not just being deaf, but having to fight all the emotions that he felt inside when he had to turn around to look at the audience when they applauded, because he could not hear them. (Source: Disabled World – http://www.disabled-world.com/artman/publish/famous-deaf.shtml)

- **Agatha Christie** (September 15, 1890 – January 12, 1976) – the world's bestselling book writer of all time, only truly surpassed by the Bible and equalled by Shakespeare. A British novelist, she has sold approximately four billion copies worldwide. Christie suffered from dyslexia but in no way did it stop her from being creative and learning how to write. Her mystery novels have always been some of the most captivating of all time. Her bestselling book is 'And Then There Was None', which continued to be a source of inspiration for novelists and movie makers even many years after her death. (Source: Disabled World – http://www.disabled-world.com/artman/publish/article_2130.shtml)

- **Danny Glover** (born July 22, 1947) – an American actor in films like the Lethal Weapon series with Mel Gibson and Predator 2. Danny Glover suffered dyslexia at school and school staff labelled him as retarded. This was not very encouraging for him but he ended up finding ways to feel better about himself. He says that dyslexia had given him the feeling that he was not worthy to learn and that the people around him did not care what would happen to his education. With time he regained his self esteem and became a great actor. (Source: Disabled World –

http://www.disabled-world.com/artman/publish/article_2130.shtml)

- **Hans Christian Andersen** (April 2, 1805 – August 4, 1875) – a Danish author of children's fantasy stories, Andersen was a victim of dyslexia and showed the world that when you really want something, nothing can stop you from obtaining it. The books that he wrote have been translated into hundreds of different languages and continue to be distributed in millions of copies today. Andersen wrote books such as 'The Emperor's New Clothes', 'The Princess and the Pea', 'Thumbelina', 'The Snow Queen', 'The Ugly Duckling' and 'The Little Mermaid'. (Source: Disabled World – http://www.disabled-world.com/artman/publish/article_2130.shtml)

- **Whoopi Goldberg** (born November 13, 1955) – an American actress, comedian, radio host, TV personality, game show host, and author. Goldberg was born Caryn Elaine Johnson in New York City. She had a lot of difficulty in school, but did not know that she had dyslexia until her adult years. Despite her dyslexia, Goldberg has had a highly successful film and television career. (Source: Disabled World –

http://www.disabled-world.com/artman/publish/article_2130.shtml)

- **Stephen Hawking** (born January 8, 1942 in Oxford, England) – a theoretical physicist, cosmologist and author.

Hawking recalls: "It was a great shock to me to discover that I had motor neurone disease. I had never been very well coordinated physically as a child. I was not good at ball games, and my handwriting was the despair of my teachers. Maybe for this reason, I didn't care much for sport or physical activities. But things seemed to change when I went to Oxford, at the age of 17. I took up coxing and rowing. I was not Boat Race standard, but I got by at the level of inter-College competition."

In his third year at Oxford, Hawking noticed that he was getting more "clumsy". He says: "I fell over once or twice for no apparent reason. But it was not until I was at Cambridge, in the following year, that my father noticed, and took me to the family doctor. He referred me to a specialist, and shortly after my 21st birthday I went into hospital for tests. I was in for two weeks, during which I had a wide variety of tests. They took a muscle sample from my arm, stuck electrodes into me, and injected some fluid into my spine, and watched it going up and down with x-rays, as they tilted the bed. After all that, they didn't tell me what I had, except that it was not multiple sclerosis, and that I was a typical case. I gathered, however, that they expected it to continue to get worse, and that there was nothing they could do, except give me vitamins. I could see that they didn't expect them to have much effect. I didn't feel like asking for more details, because they were obviously bad."

When Hawking realised that he had a form of disease that was incurable, that the disease was likely to kill him in a few years, he was shocked. He questioned how something like this could happen to him, wondering why he should suffer in such a manner. Initially, Hawking did not know what was going to happen to him because of his disability; how it would progress was uncertain. He has had motor neurone disease for most of his adult life, but it has not prevented him from having a family and a successful job. He attributes his success to the assistance he received from his first wife, Jane, as well as from his children, and large numbers of people and organisations. "I have been lucky, that my condition has progressed more slowly than is often the case. But it shows that one need not lose hope," says Hawking. (Source: Disabled World – www.disabled-world.com)

- **Dorothy Miles** (Dorothy May Miles, August 19, 1931 – January 30, 1993). Dorothy Miles was the youngest of five surviving children. She contracted cerebrospinal meningitis, which left her deaf, in 1939. She was educated at the Royal School for the Deaf and the Mary Hare School. In 1957, aged 25, Miles went to the Gallaudet College in America. Some of the sponsorship was provided by the British Deaf and Dumb Association (now known as the British Deaf Association – BDA). In 1961 she graduated with a BA degree with distinction. While at the Gallaudet College she edited magazines and won prizes for writing prose and poems, and for acting. She returned to the UK in 1977. On her return she pioneered programmes such as the 'See Hear' television series for the deaf. She worked on various projects with the BDA, compiled the first BSL teaching manual for teachers and was involved in setting up the Council for the Advancement of Communication with Deaf People (CACDP), now known as Signature. Miles is regarded as an important person in the literary heritage of sign language and the deaf community.

Further information

Some names and website addresses of organisations providing training and information for the deaf and disabled communities.

Action for Hearing Loss (formerly RNID)

www.actiononhearingloss.org.uk

Royal National Institute of Blind People (RNIB)

www.rnib.org.uk

Royal Association for Deaf People (RAD)

www.royaldeaf.org.uk

British Deaf Association (BDA)

www.bda.org.uk

Remark!

www.remark.uk.com

British Dyslexia Association (BDA)

www.bdadyslexia.org.uk

About the Author

Joy Ani is a Sunday school teacher, the author of 'Help My Heart', the founder and leader of 'Let's Talk About the Bible' Bible club, and an evangelist. She graduated from the School of Disciples where she discovered a whole new passion for soul winning. Her greatest desire is to share the Word of Truth with a dying world. She has a BA (Hons) in Human Resources and Retail Management. Joy is married to Fidelis and they are blessed with three wonderful children.

To contact the author or purchase other great books please visit: www.seeknfindstores.co.uk.

We stock an exceptional range of inspirational Christian books, Bibles, CDs, DVDs, games and gift items for adults and children. For more information please visit our online bookstore at: www.seeknfindstores.co.uk. We are open 24 hours a day, seven days a week. Email us at: info@seeknfindstores.co.uk

www.ingramcontent.com/pod-product-compliance
Lightning Source LLC
Chambersburg PA
CBHW050554300426
44112CB00013B/1909